RANDOM THR

Volume II

High Streets & Hedgerows

Alex I. Askaroff

Other titles by the same author:

Random Threads Volume I
Patches of Heaven

Random Threads Volume II
Skylark Country

Random Threads Volume III
High Streets & Hedgerows

Books published containing the author's work:

A Celebration of Childhood, Rivacre, Paperback
Natural Peace, Anchor Books, Paperback
Poetry of Kent, Millfield, Paperback
This Natural World, Arrival Press, Hardback
South East Poets, Arrival Press, Hardback
Let's do Lunch, Remus new fiction, Paperback
Anchor Poets, Anchor Books, Hardback
This Vanishing World, Poetry Now, Hardback
Web of Thoughts, Anchor Books, Hardback
The Good Ol' Days, Arrival Press, Hardback
New Rhymes for Children, Arrival Press, Hardback
A Tapestry of Thoughts, Spotlight, Paperback
Mixed Musings, Poetry Now, Hardback
Special Occasions, Arrival Press, Hardback

RANDOM THREADS
Volume III

High Streets
&
Hedgerows

By
Alex I. Askaroff
©2002

Crows Nest Publications
www.sussexsewingmachines.com
www.crowsnestpublications.com

Crows Nest Publications
148 Willingdon Park Drive,
Eastbourne
East Sussex
England
BN22 0DG

First Edition

Paperback ISBN
0-9539410-3-5

CIP library reference: **Nostalgia**
First published in Great Britain in 2002

Printed by
Tansleys Printers
Seaford
East Sussex

For more information on how to order this book visit our websites @

www.sussexsewingmachines.com
www.crowsnestpublications.com

Introduction

Meet my good friend Alex through the medium of his books and you will be refreshed by his enthusiasm and great affection for all that is described between the covers.

You will find that he **repairs sewing machines in East Sussex** – a mundane daily routine you might think but the owners of many are often in the remotest and beautiful corners of our beloved county. He traverses hills and marshes, lanes and tracks, through woodlands, along valleys; he soaks up the views of seascapes, estuaries, harbours and rivers, around the glorious Downs and the Sussex Weald. His journeys are presented to you with fulsome description of the great pleasure he derives from travelling through our lovely countryside and with much humour in his anecdotal references to his visits.

You may feel that you know **East Sussex** but I will guarantee that Alex provokes you into wanting to look again and just in case you cannot manage it physically he will fill your minds with the happiest of thoughts which will be refreshed every time you turn a page.

Alex loves his life, his family, his animals, his environment, his vocation and, as you read on, be certain that you will share the warmth with which his books are written.

Frank Scutt OBE

CONTENTS

Acknowledgements

This is the third and final book in the Random Threads trilogy. It has been a great pleasure to write and although it may have driven most of my family mad whilst writing it, I have enjoyed every second. Once again I have thrown way too many adjectives and verbs to the wind, but that is part of my writing, it comes from the heart. That is one of the wonderful benefits of self-publishing *having the final word.*

The third and final book sounds like the end of the road for my colourful travels. This if far from the truth, I am sure that a new series of books will rise from the blank pages of my computer before long.

Self-publishing is an enormous amount of work, I assembled a fantastic team to work closely with me throughout the book. After the third book one would think that it gets easier, well, it **does not** it is just a huge amount of work. I would say that writing the book is only about 50%, the rest is publishing from editing to printing. A big thank you goes to my team, assembled for one sole purpose of bringing this book to life.

I must thank all the people that have made this series possible. Firstly, of course is Yana, my wife, who puts up with me and makes all things possible. My best and worst critic, without her not a word would have been written.

Many thanks goes to Stevie for once again sitting down and ploughing through my work. The Ripley family even had to put up with my manuscript and my son on their holiday. Stevie, they are two small words but I really mean them, *thank you.*

Many thanks goes to Lin Hall in Queensland, Australia, who spent such a lot of time and effort in trying, sometimes in vain, to teach me English. Lin also really knocked the book into shape for me, something that I am eternally grateful for. Lin, *thank you mate.*

Thanks to Amanda, Andy, Peter and all at Tansley's the printers. They have been incredible with their input, I would recommend them to anyone.

Now, I must thank Diane Peachey in Savannah, America, for coming up with such a lovely title. Diane won our competition for the title that had several hundred entries. When I saw her title it was spot on and I fell in love with it straight away.

Finally, thanks to so many of you that took the time to e-mail me with your comments on the first two books. I have received over a thousand e-mails and saved 60 pages crammed with your wonderful remarks, if one thing spurred me on to complete the trilogy it was the unsolicited support of complete strangers who filled my heart with words of encouragement and support.

Thank you all.

ALEX I ASKAROFF

Our lives are often remembered by the gifts that we leave our children. Well Sarah and Tom, this book, my memories, my thoughts and my words, are my gift to you.

Love Dad

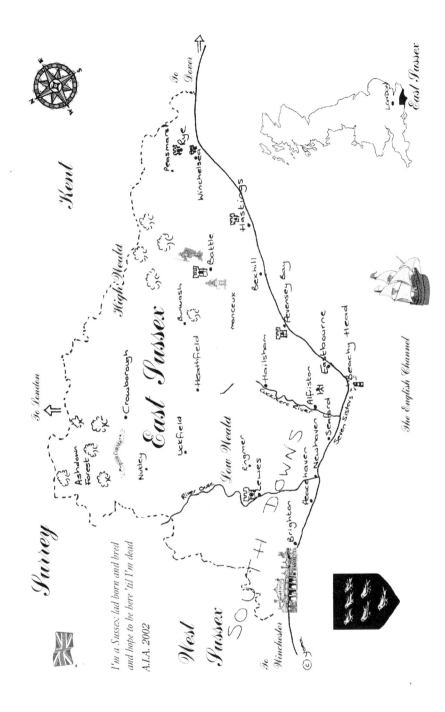

Surrey

Kent

West Sussex

East Sussex

*I'm a Sussex lad born and bred
and hope to be here 'til I'm dead*
A.I.A. 2002

High Weald

Low Weald

SOUTH DOWNS

Ashdown Forest

Crowborough

Nutley

Uckfield

Ringmer

Lewes

River Ouse

Peacehaven

Newhaven

Brighton

Seaford

Alfriston

Hailsham

Heathfield

Burwash

Battle

Bexhill

Manceux

Hastings

Winchelsea

Rye

Peasmarsh

Pevensey Bay

Eastbourne

Seven Sisters

Beachy Head

To London

To Dover

To Winchester

The English Channel

London

East Sussex

© John

Author's Note

When people think of England, everyone knows we are different. I mean, only the English would expect the 6000 other languages around the globe to learn our tongue so that we can speak English wherever we go.

You know that old saying about *mad dogs and Englishmen*? Well we all know it's true. Thoughts of batty vicars rushing around the churchyard and old school mistresses in chequered blazers, teaching hockey, spring to mind. People have visions of old bangers clogging up the roads and 10-mile queues of traffic following an old biddy on her bicycle. Of eccentric country gentlemen shooting pheasant and peasants in equal numbers.

England summons up images of cricket on the green, afternoon teas, salmon and cucumber sandwiches, church bells ringing on Saturday afternoon for the parish wedding, choir boys singing Christmas carols and of baked potatoes on bonfire night, gymkhanas and village fayres. Of bowlers in pristine white outfits on bowling greens that are so perfect they look like they have been manicured and each blade of grass trimmed with nail clippers.

You cannot but mention England and people will say how polite we all are. At one of my schools after being smacked with the shiniest plimsoll that ever existed, we were taught to stand up and say *thank you* to our teacher, something that to this day I will never understand. I used to leave the room grinning at the ridiculousness of it all. Once the teacher heard me laughing in the corridor after my punishment, called me back and walloped me again. I had to say *thank you* – twice!

England brings visions of Girl Guides and Boy Scouts, of fish and chips eaten out of yesterday's newspapers smothered in salt and vinegar and endless rainy days. Mental pictures burst forth of locals gossiping in village pubs that have served strange sounding brews like *Speckled Hen* or *Indian Pale Ale* for a hundred years.

Then there are the annual flower shows, fayres and fêtes, Women's Institute raffles, Salvation Army bands and Chelsea Pensioners parading in their red uniforms up and down the main street at every opportunity. You have the Horse Guards trotting up the Mall to Buckingham Palace, red double-decker buses and London black cabs. Tattooed football hooligans, with shaved heads and earrings, that look like they eat children and razor blades for breakfast but cry like babies when the national anthem is played.

These are but a few images of England and amazingly, they still survive, every one of them. Well, except the country gentleman shooting peasants, he lost his gun licence and has taken up pike fishing.

Another point is the English are renowned for their betting. Not just on horses or the dogs, but on just about anything that can run, jump, stick or whistle – from wellie-tossing to cherry-stone spitting, from conker bashing to throwing horseshoes. We will bet our shirts on anything, from who will win the next boat race, to the possibility of Elvis serving up our fish 'n' chips. Betting is a national pastime and those of us who don't bet still do! We pretend we are having the occasional little *flutter* that could never be construed as **betting**. Then we shoot down to the *Nags Head* or the *Rat and Parrot* to drown our sorrows over a pint – or six – of bitter-smelling liquid that most people would not let their kitchen sink swallow.

I think the Queen is probably the most well known person on our planet. We may all recognise our mothers but the world recognizes our monarch. You could show her picture anywhere on this earth and people would grin in recognition. The funny thing is that, while the rest of the world has these quaint pictures of England, people living here most definitely **do not**.

I have said this many times before but if I had a pound for every person who I had met that has told me *things ain't like they used to be* I would be in Monte Carlo right now throwing black jacks in a casino, laughing each time I lost and lighting cigars with twenty-pound notes. The plain fact is that these images are true. Wars, rationing and a host of horrible diseases from *the good old days* are gone but essentially England is much the same as she always has been.

What the people in our larger towns do not realise is that they have encircled themselves in concrete, asphalt and 24-hour noise. The countryside, the real England, is still there. The only difference is that you have to look for it. There was no nuclear winter, no meteorite disaster. England did not disappear under a tidal wave sometime in the spring of 1959, she just evolved. People can no longer look out of their windows and expect to see a gaggle of geese going off to market. Modern England is still the home of tennis, cricket, rugby and golf and, while the rest of the world may beat us at the games that we invented, it is not to say that we do not still relish them.

To make my point, there were about a million or so Morris 1000 saloon cars made back in the '50s and '60s and something like 80% are still on our roads doodling along. Yana, my wife, drives hers almost every day, it is nearly 40 years old and still runs beautifully. The majority of these English oddities and eccentricities are still flourishing. The milkman can still be heard at four in the morning whining along the road in his electric milk float, bottles clinking. Packets of tea and soap powder samples still drop through my letterbox with the regularity of an atomic clock, delivered by postmen on their red bicycles.

England is still a beautiful country. Today there is still nowhere in the world where you could find a landscape more ravishing and traditions as rich than in East Sussex. I know there are places of such beauty here that my words lay heavy upon their splendour. East Sussex represents much of the real beauty of rural England with its wonderful downland, ancient woodland and wetlands it is still a place of mystery, dreams and adventure.

Our rich pastimes are, in spite of every modern convenience, still here for all who seek them. It has been my blessing to have been born into such a full and diverse culture and realise it while I was still young enough to embrace it.

Writing always feels like a slightly unbalanced pastime for me. I am usually such a busy energetic person who has a family to bring up, a house and gardens to maintain, two businesses to run and a million things to do from sunrise to sunset. I am a man of many hobbies – from wood and metal turning to fishing and cycling to simply walking the dog or gardening on a sunny afternoon. All are sacrificed to the written word.

To write and publish my books I have to shut myself away in forced isolation. Motionless except for my fingers tapping away at computer keys. Outside the world still turns. I catch glimpses of my children returning home. The dog runs by the study doorway chasing one of our cats. The sun

– sets but I do not realise it. All things move but not me, the complete opposite of my normal life. Isolation becomes the writer's norm.

What makes it all possible is one simple thing: my love for creating something that can transcend time. My books are a joy to write. The people and places that I visit are captured on paper and shared with the world. I have in my own little way made a time capsule. In writing I do the one thing that cannot be done with my life, freeze time. I try to capture East Sussex and its inhabitants and seal them away between the pages of these books where they can remain, ageless.

On average it takes me almost a year to complete one book, hence this trilogy has taken three years of my spare time, my hobbies and friends' time. Has it been worth it? The answer to that is a simple yes. To create something as I have done many times in wood or metal is always a joy. Now I have created something on paper that fills me with more pride than any of my other creations. I can honestly say that the Random Threads trilogy has been a pleasure to craft.

In my work, I have travelled the high streets and hedgerows of the towns and countryside in my area. This book, the last in the Random Threads trilogy, is another snippet from my daily life. A peek into the world in which I live and the place in which I grew. Enjoy!

Alex I Askaroff

www.sussexsewingmachines.com   Email: alexsussex@aol.com
www.crowsnestpublications.com

CABBAGES & CAKES

I was still half-asleep as my eyes started to focus, but all was not well. I looked down again, with a quizzical look, trying to concentrate my blurred vision. That can't be right? I was scratching my un-brushed head, staring down over the front of my *Homer Simpson* pyjamas, to my feet. I was standing on the dreaded scales!

What had made me drag them out of the larder was anybody's guess. Perhaps I had an idea that all was not well in the weight division. I had no idea how serious the situation was. I was temporarily frozen to the spot as the horrendous scales spat out their findings.

It must be a mistake? I stood on my left foot, that altered the scales slightly, but in the wrong direction. Then I tried balancing on my right foot. The scales still hovered around the 15-stone mark. I then picked up the scales and whizzed them left to right, like a frantic rally-car driver on hairpin bends, watching the dial of the scales spin like a top and come to a rocking-rest back on zero. I confidently put them back on the kitchen floor with renewed optimism.

There was no doubt that I had now shaken the dust out of the springs, or whatever it was inside that was **obviously** faulty. Now that they had been taught who was the boss, they were bound to work properly. I went to stand on them again but hesitated, just for a second. A thought ran through my sleepy brain but it was soon dismissed, there was no way I could have put on two stone without realising…could I?

By now I was wide-awake. The morning muzzy head I had woken up with was crystal clear. I stood in silence, summoning up all my mind control to work on the scales, I even pulled my belly in, like a private on parade, *chest out, chin up*. Surely that would help a bit?

I stepped up to the scales like a condemned man to the scaffold. The scales shot round and the awful number 15 came up to the thin red line. It shook for a second before coming to rest as if it was having a good laugh. I jumped off as if electrocuted! Still shocked I looked around to make sure no one had seen me. I heard Yana coming down the stairs; perhaps she had not noticed my expanding waistline. Mum's the word. I quickly pushed the scales back into the kitchen larder and went about finishing off my morning cup of tea.

I was nonchalantly stirring my tea when Yana walked in. "Oh, Yana, when you are in town today do you think you could buy a new pair of scales? I think ours are a bit outdated. Buy one of those new digital ones that are guaranteed accurate. You know the sort."
"What's wrong with the old ones?" Yana asked suspiciously.
"Oh, I think they have seized up a bit, you know what those old mechanical ones are like, anyway they are never that accurate..."
"Alex," Yana laughed knowingly, "had a bit of a shock haven't you!"
"What do you mean?" I spouted indignantly, keeping my stomach firmly pulled in and marching around the dining room in my colourful jim-jams. "You know exactly what I mean, one cake too many. One old dear too far! One digestive biscuit, one cream cake, one *'Oh I'll just have another cup of coffee'*, too much! That's what I mean. All those customers, all of those little snacks, eh? Now its payback time"
"You never said anything!" I said frantically. "Why didn't you tell me? For God sake what am I going to do?" I sat and dropped my head despairingly into my hands.
"Calm down – you don't look too bad. Maybe you are right, maybe those old scales are wrong. It must be a good year since you last weighed yourself. I will get some new scales today and you can weigh yourself again at lunchtime."

I went off to work without eating breakfast. In my mind I was analysing the last year. It had been a good one, a prosperous one. The business had really settled down. It was a big change from the early days when we started the business. The days when we did not know where our next meal was coming from. Those days of long hours and little money were almost forgotten. Now I had regular customers and bookings for days, sometimes weeks ahead. I had security, and that breeds complacency. Yana was right, I had stopped and chatted to customers that, over the years, had become friends. I loved the sound of the kettle boiling and a cup of hot coffee appearing with some biscuits perched on the side of the saucer.

I racked my brains looking for someone, beside myself, that I could blame. There must be someone to blame… Someone or something.

Ah yes, I know, it's my trousers! The super-comfortable Marks & Spencers corduroy trousers with the Lycra content that allowed my waist to silently enlarge – without the traditional painful signals. There was none of that-strangulated, garrotted, feeling that I used to get when my jeans would no longer yield to the pressure of my expanding belly. That was the sign that I had always used. The sign to cut down on my food consumption.

I drove on, feeling slightly better at having found the culprit of my present dilemma. But as the morning wore on, I became apprehensive about lunch time. I started to hope that Yana had failed in her attempt to buy the new scales. Perhaps the whole of Eastbourne had sold out of them? There was always a chance, wasn't there?

I was in denial. Hoping against all odds that the inevitable show down could somehow be postponed.

By lunchtime I was starving. I had politely refused every offer of drinks and sustenance throughout the entire morning. Even the superb apricot Victoria sponge from old Edna in Hellingly was painfully refused. I almost dribbled as she took it away. I was not sure who was the most upset! Mind you, her enormously overweight golden retriever eagerly followed her out to the kitchen. At least *the mutt* would be in for a treat!

The morning had lasted the equivalent of two normal days. It was like being back in the school classroom, in the class of the most boring teacher, watching the clock laboriously tick round, every hour seeming like two.

I sat in the Land Rover outside my home for a few moments. There were a few options, leave quietly and make some excuse to Yana. Just get on the scales and then tuck into a big, well-deserved lunch. Or – I could face the music. I decided that at least the third option held the promise of food at the end of it. By now even a lettuce-sandwich sounded appealing. With a rumbling belly I walked into the house. On the kitchen floor was my nemesis. A brand new set of Salter digital scales.

"They are the most expensive scales I could find," Yana said as she saw me looking ominously down at them. "Guaranteed to be 99% accurate."

I wondered how it was possible to hate something that was not even alive. Something that I had never met before and that had never done anyone any harm.

"Right! Well done! They look - err-fine, thanks Yana."

Thanks for what? Why did I ask her to buy them in the first place? Why was I about to inflict such pain on myself? I looked in the mirror. If I stood side-on and held my breath just right I did not look much different than before. I pulled my belly in and then let it out, in-out, in-out, before and after.

It was no good I was going to have to get on the scales. I pressed the side of the scales and stepped on them. I had my eyes tightly closed and counted to five, then looked down with one eye.

"What the! 15 stone and six pounds. That's 216 pounds! How the hell can that be possible?" I turned and caught Yana trying to smother her laughter in the dining room. "What's so funny eh? I am dying here, I need sympathy and consolation not sniggering."
"Try taking some of your clothes off!"
"Ah, good idea."

I stripped to my boxer shorts. I even removed my socks, *they must weigh a good few ounces*, I thought. I stood back on the piece of plastic junk that had made me hate it with venom in five seconds flat.

"Fifteen stone and three pounds," I exclaimed, "that's still more than the old mechanical scales said this morning, and I have not eaten a thing! I think I need to reweigh myself on those ones, just to make sure."

I slipped the old scales along the floor with my foot and stood on them. At least I found with the mechanical ones you could get a slightly better reading if you adopted a ballet-like pose, one foot diagonally across the scales, arms high in the air.

I was totally engrossed in the middle of my examination when there came a tap on the window. Gary, from Parcel Force, was beaming at me through the kitchen window, holding up a box and pointing to it. The smug grin on his face told me he had seen my whole performance and was only just managing to control himself. I immediately struck a manly pose and pointed to the side door. Seconds later I heard Gary and Yana killing themselves with laughter. I was not amused. I saw Gary walking back up the path. He turned with a grin and gave me the *thumbs-up* sign. I sort of waved back, hobbling trying to get my left leg back into my trousers.

"It's all so funny for you isn't it?" I said to Yana as I sat at the dining table. "Here I am, starving to death and dying of thirst and you're just having a laugh with Postman Pat!"
"Oh don't be so moody! I have fixed you a nice salad for your lunch. All you have to do is cut down slowly and all that weight will disappear." Yana pushed a bowl of lettuce in front of me. "Now doesn't that look lovely and colourful?"
"Yeah – it would do if it had a slab of chicken on top." I moaned back as I tried to eat the first leaf of the wretched stuff.
"Get used to it big boy, because this is just the start. My friend is sending me over the *cabbage diet*. It is supposed to be so good you can lose seven pounds a week and eat as much of it as you like."

I slunk off to the kettle, at least I was going to have a nice cup of tea and sod the sugar. I was going to enjoy it like a red wine at the *Last Supper*. I had to almost force the lettuce salad down. Even hungry I could not see what rabbits saw in it. My mind started to go all sneaky and a plan was emerging.
"Yana, of course you know – it is all down to brain power."
"What are you talking about?"
"My weight, it's all down to mind-over-matter."
"Oh, so you can lose weight just by thinking about it?"
"Of course, shall I prove it?"
"I would like to see you try."
"OK, let's do a deal. I am pretty sure that I can lose about half my weight immediately, just by using the outstanding ability of my enormous brain power."
"Alex, sometimes you are just full of it. You know as well as I do that it's impossible!"
"Well, if it's impossible you have nothing to lose have you? I will make it

really simple. If I don't lose the weight I will cook you a full English breakfast, in bed tomorrow morning with all the works, including marmalade and toast. If you lose, you do the same for me, OK?"

"Let me just get this straight, you are going to stand on those bathroom scales and lose weight, right now, with both feet on the scales and not holding onto anything?"

"Yes, I don't see that as a problem to someone of my capabilities."

"Then *Mr smarty pants*, you have yourself a deal."

I rose slowly from the table with a look of pure concentration, moving slowly towards the scales that were still on the kitchen floor. "Wait just one moment, I need to mentally prepare myself for this."

I started a low chanting hum, like a witch doctor around a fire. As the pitch rose I summoned up all my powers. I slowly moved my left foot onto the mechanical scales, then, in a flash, put my right foot onto the electronic ones. I spurted out in a triumphant voice. "See the scales are reading less than eight stone each!"

"You cheating dog, that's not allowed," snapped Yana.

"Why? I have both feet on the scales. You didn't say it had to be **the same scales**. I am standing, just as I predicted, on the scales – at half the weight! I pronounce myself the undisputed winner. Oh, and that will be two slices of bacon and two eggs tomorrow!"

I walked defiantly back to my cup of tea. "A bet is a bet." I added "And that will teach you to laugh at me with the postman."

"Well," said Yana, "tomorrow you can call breakfast the last meal of a condemned man because, after that, you are on *the cabbage diet*." Yana smiled, as if she was going to get some evil pleasure out of watching me suffer day after day.

The breakfast was fit for a king. Yana and I tucked into a full English, sitting in bed. The fried tomatoes slipped down and the mushrooms tossed in butter simply exuded aroma. The dry cured, best-back bacon filled the house with an irresistible smell and the local farm-made sausages, well, they were *to die* for. I dipped each slice into Heinz tomato ketchup before devouring them. I stuffed myself, putting all thoughts of my oncoming diet well to the back of my mind as another slice of toast with butter and marmalade was washed down with a second cup of English breakfast tea.

I went to work as happy as a lark. My belly sloshing around like a full beer barrel. Come lunchtime the first bowl of cabbage soup was quite appealing. I even had a second bowl. This was going to be a good diet – no problem at all. I was almost looking forward to a visit to the scales the following week, to announce my seven-pound loss to the world.

But, as with all diets, things did not go according to plan. By the second day of the diet, even the smell of cabbage made me feel ill. The bowl that was so lovingly placed in front of me, by my smirking wife, was full of dread. I came to hate it.

By the sixth day I was like a starving, depraved, Humphrey Bogart, lost in some infernal jungle, dying for one good meal. Just the thought of that rancid bowl of jungle-juice turned a mild-mannered man into a beast. I roamed the streets at night, with Rolly, my faithful mutt, eagerly pulling on the lead in the lamplight. All just to avoid going near the wretched cabbage soup. The only hope, the only light at the end of an endless dark tunnel, was the seventh and final day of the diet. That day was my only salvation, my only reason for living. After what was the longest week of my life, I once more pulled the scales from the larder and placed them on the kitchen floor.

I had been good. As anybody that has been on a serious diet will understand, the hunger pangs are terrible. It is a matter of pure will-power not to succumb. Yana had hidden all sources of temptation from me and I had survived seven days of hell. I stood for a while looking down, once more, at my nemesis. I felt weak and miserable, with no energy. If someone had told me I was to be taken out and shot I would have hardly flinched.

I held my breath and, with Yana apprehensively watching, I stood upon the digital scales. They were blank for a moment then maliciously flashed up the numbers. I could not control myself, I screamed "15 stone and 4 bloody pounds," "that's not #!*#*?$ possible! How the *!~#?&* can that be right? I knew those new fangled digital scales were *&$#!*. I got back on them again as I must have read them wrong, I hadn't. Furious and red-faced, my verbal onslaught continued unabated as I released a series of expletives towards the hapless scales that lay impassively on the floor ignoring my abuse.

Yana looked on with silent astonishment. She had heard more swear words in 10 seconds than in the last 25 years of our marriage. My lack of energy was replaced with a rush of wild blood. I suddenly found that nothing returns the energy quicker than rage… take my word for it. I was a man possessed.

I grabbed the scales, ran out of the house and in one single movement, flung them as far as I could. I watched as they glided, almost majestically, over the fence towards my neighbour's conservatory. Realising what I had done I watched in wide-eyed horror as the scales, thrown with a sudden surge of Olympic strength, headed straight at the glass panels on the side of their pride and joy. To my relief the scales hit the stone-supporting wall, just a few inches below the glass and exploded into a hundred pieces, the bits dropped like missiles into the long grass and all went quiet.

"Well, so much for the *wonder diet*!" I said to Yana as she came running out of the house. "I have starved for a week, even had trouble walking. I could hardly remember where I lived I was so exhausted! And for all that I have put on a pound!"
"You look slimmer, it must be fluid." Yana said trying to console me, "And as a celebration, I bought you one of your favourite cakes."
"Thank God for that!" I said as we walked back inside. We looked at each other and burst out laughing.

After a huge slice of the best-tasting cake ever made and a good mug of piping-hot coffee, we made a plan. I was to just slowly cut down on my intake of food and lose the weight gradually. It would become my mission for the year. I would try and stick to it as best I could. I would try hard to resist all the cream cakes and afternoon teas, all the homemade biscuits and little *perks* of the job. Yana, in turn, agreed never to give me cabbage soup again. As for the scales, well they would never be 99% of anything, ever again and a good thing too.

That night, under the cover of darkness, I crept into my neighbour's garden like an SAS commando. I removed all the evidence I could find of the scales and then examined the brickwork with my tiny torch. I brushed away a few bits of plastic that had lodged in the brickwork and made my escape. I made sure that I left no evidence of my discus-throwing attempt of a few hours earlier, then slipped away into the night.

DIAMONDS ARE FOREVER

The traffic was snarling up and I was running late, again. It is amazing how het up and frustrated we all get waiting in queues. It does not matter what kind of queue, but a traffic jam is one of the worst. By the time I arrived at my next call I was running 35 minutes late, hungry and dying of thirst. My compulsive slimming diet had a lot to answer for.

As I pressed the door bell I mentally prepared myself for a bit of a scalding. Old women have a natural way of telling you off without having to say a word, just a glance is sometimes all it needs. I had visions of being turned to stone with a fiery stare when the door opened. Instead of a cold welcome, a small, pleasant man with a broad smile greeted me.

"Come in young man, we have been expecting you."
"I am so sorry I am late," I started but he cut in.
"No matter, we are not in a hurry, sometimes it is just better to let life go at its own pace."

I smiled to myself as I walked over the threshold, almost immediately calming down. I followed the old man down the corridor towards his living room when he stopped and pointed to a picture on the wall.

"Sixty-three years, eh, 63 years married to the same girl and I was not too sure we would be together till the end of our first year."

Walter was pointing proudly at the picture of the Queen and a letter that she had written to Irene and Walter to celebrate their diamond wedding. The Queen was smiling down from the gilt frame in one of her usual serene, *royal* poses.

"Well, what's your secret then Walter? How have you lasted 63 years when today most couples seem to be getting divorced the week after their honeymoon?"
"Ah, it's all in communicating and doing things together – not apart – together. Mind you, back in the early days I can't say that I thought we were going to be together for long. We were married on the same day that World War II broke out. I remember the family sitting in the living room

and chatting about the wedding when my father interrupted us and turned the radio up. The war came as a bit of a shock back in '39. We knew things were bad, but not that bad! At the local *flicks* we all saw Chamberlain coming off the plane shaking that piece of paper with all the signatures on it. *Peace in our time* and all that! Got that a bit wrong didn't he? We were married for a whole day of peacetime."

"Back in September of 1939 Irene and I were happy as larks. Our wedding had gone as planned. We had put down a £30 deposit on a lovely new semi-detached being built in Dartford. I was on less than £5 a week, so £30 was a lot, almost two months work. We even chose the fireplace and the kitchen. The builders did a lovely job on the house. It was going to be the perfect family home. Well, that did not last long! Before I knew it I was chasing Rommel all over North Africa in Pye-Core. Irene was at home with a baby on the way and all hell was breaking loose."

"Things then went from bad to worse. Irene had only been in the house six months when the mortgage lenders chucked us out of our lovely new home. It was because we could not pay the mortgage on a private's army wage. They never even gave us our deposit back! That was a deep cut to us. I remember an old saying about banks. *They are the first to give you an umbrella when it's dry and the first to take it away again when it starts to rain.* Well, anyway, shortly after that Irene had our son and no home. Luckily my father bought up an old house at the end of a street that had been left to rot a bit. All he had to do was pay off the loan on it and the lady living there let him have it. Irene had to move from her lovely, spick-n-span home to an old ramshackle of a house that needed completely gutting to make it fit for a baby to live in."

Irene took over the conversation in one seamless motion polished from 63 years of practice. "Within 12 months we had gone from having a bright future to fighting for our lives. Walter was all over the desert, sometimes chasing and sometimes being chased by the *Desert Fox* and I was watching bombers drop their loads over London. The moonlit nights were the worst, as the planes could see the Thames glowing in the night. They would follow it right up to the city. We had Ack-Ack guns on Bexley Heath and Dartford Common. That would be bad news as well! For as soon as the guns opened up on the bombers they would see the flashes and drop their loads all over us."

"If that was not bad enough, towards the end of the war, Doodlebugs began falling from the sky. God, how we hated those devils! When they first started we did not know what they were. They turned out to be howling demons, riding a whirlwind of death! The World Shop, that used to supply just about everything we needed, where we exchanged our weekly ration vouchers for food, was one of the first to be hit. Killed so many that one bomb! Terrible. Just terrible!"

"Nothing we could do about it, we just carried on as best as we could. We would hear later whose house had been hit or which street had been blown up. When you heard a bomb coming you would just pray that the *Bug* would not stop."

"Awful when you think about it. But if it went by, then you knew you were safe. The worst time was the night bombings. They would start around 2 am. The sirens wailing in the night sky would wake you up and I would have to grab my son and rush for the Anderson shelter in the garden. The neighbours did not have a shelter so they crammed in with me. We would just sit there in the pitch dark – guns blasting away, bombs dropping – just hoping that our name was not on one of the bombs."

"The worst thing about the shelter was the beetles. Can you imagine huddling in the dark, clutching a crying baby, with the terrible thunder raging outside and crawly, little black beetles creeping all over your feet and up your legs? Nothing we could do about it. During the day there was not a single beetle in sight. Maybe they were as scared as we were? Still I did hate those little beasts."

"There were some funny times as well. We all talk about it now, the few of us that are still left. The camaraderie was something special. We were all friends, even complete strangers, we all pulled together, hoping for a brighter future."

Walter jumped into the conversation. "Remember that time – back in '42 was it, or maybe '43, when I was stationed at the barracks up the road?" "Oh yes, that was funny." Irene continued. "Walter had worked his way up to Lance Corporal so the money was getting better and, even though he was only 20 miles away, leave was out of the question. They were just regrouping before being shipped back out to North Africa."

"Well, one day, one of the personnel carriers dropped one of its tracks and had to be repaired. Walter took the opportunity to oversee the repairs and make sure they went smoothly. All the rest of the group had gone off on exercises for the day, so much of the camp was empty. Walter had a brainwave. To test the carrier, just to make sure the tracks were repaired properly you see, he got the driver to head straight up to Dartford to see me. What a sight! What a noise! The whole town thought the invasion had begun and the Germans were coming. People were rushing everywhere."

"I came out to see what all the commotion was about. I could see Walter waving as the carrier slid around the bottom of the road. The machine ground along the street and at the end, the driver slammed on the brakes, locked up the left track, then put his foot down, full throttle on the other track. It spun the machine on a sixpence. He then came to a grinding halt, rocking, outside the front door in a cloud of smoke. We had tea and sandwiches and a lovely hour before they had to make the street shake again and get back to camp. If Walter was caught it would have been a serious reprimand but, as it was, it worked out just fine."

"Towards the end of the war, when Walter was busy chasing fifth columnists out of Persia, the troops started to arrive home. You always knew when someone's husband was arriving back as they would hang flags all down the street and around the house. Oh what a special day that was for the lucky lady! We would all come out to cheer as the husband proudly walked the last few yards and received the hero's welcome. Secretly we all wished for the day that it would be our turn to see the man we loved come around the corner and know that he was here to stay."

"Then it was Walter's turn to come home. He was demobbed in '46. Alan, our son, was only six and had never really known his father, except for the occasional visit. Walter had been away fighting for the whole of Alan's young life. Walter's own father met him at Dartford railway station and splashed out on a taxi for the special journey. After all, it was Walter's homecoming."

"I shall never forget my son, waiting so eagerly by the gate, pacing up and down. The flags were all up in the street and we were all desperately waiting for a first sign of the car. It was at times like that, when a minute took an hour. At last, Walter's car arrived and Alan rushed up to him, threw his arms around him and gave him just the biggest hug a six-year-old could possibly give. It was a special moment and one I shall never forget. It still brings tears to my eyes when I think about it. The day Walter came home it was the beginning of our new life. It was as if all the horrors of those desperate, dark, early days were behind us and the future was clear and rosy."

"What a lovely story." I said, "Now I know your secret after surviving all that, marriage is a doddle."

"Yes, it put life into perspective all right, not knowing if you were going to survive one night let alone 60 years together." Said Irene clutching Walters hand and giving it a squeeze.

By the time I had finished the Singer, I had been watered and fed. My bad mood had evaporated as fast as an early summer mist and I had been told a marvellous story to boot.

When I hear about some people's struggles, just to survive, it always puts my life back into proportion. No wonder Walter did not mind me being a few minutes late. Compared to a Doodlebug dropping through the ceiling it was a minor problem.

I left Walter and Irene standing at their doorway waving me off, like an old friend. I doubted if our paths would ever cross again as Irene hardly sewed any more. But if they did, I would just love to hear more of those early years of struggle and strife. Years, that made the heart grow strong and the soul resilient. Years that built character and dignity. But, most of all, years that built a friendship between a couple that would last a lifetime.

Part of our superb coastal downland, leading to Belle Tout in the far distance. These undulations are known fondly as the Seven Sisters and each one is named. The grounds off Beachy Head have the highest number of shipwrecks per square mile in the world.

*This picture was taken during WWII. It is Sea Road, St. Leonards, they were the first line of defence
and proved a success in bringing down the flying bombs.
(With kind permission from the Imperial War Museum, London.)*

The same view today with no trace of its violent past. A much more peaceful and serene sight.

CANDLESTICKS

"I'm sorry love, I cannot understand a word you are saying," I said to the old dear staring at me from behind her front door.

She started again, this time signalling with her hand as well. She was putting something into her mouth and waving me into her home, all at the same time. I followed her and waited in the hall as she disappeared into her bedroom. She returned a few seconds later and spoke perfect English.

"Ah that's better, my teeth are in now," she said chomping up and down. "I was trying to tell you that they weren't in when you were at the door."

I just smiled back at the old dear. Her sunken face had assumed its normal shape with the help of some artificial ivory. I put my toolbox down and removed the case of the sewing machine. "What seems to be the problem Mrs Gable?" I asked as I turned the hand wheel with my practised expertise. "Just needs a service. Oh, and something went bang the last time I used it, there was a lot of smoke but that went away after I opened all the doors."

I could not help feeling that I was encountering another elderly woman with a few marbles loose. As she turned to walk across the room away from me she tripped on my toolbox sending its contents flying and made a slow lurch, head first, towards the wall. I leapt to my feet, jumped over my box and grabbed her with both hands a second before she would have head-butted the brick wall. "Are you all right Mrs Gable?" I asked through gasps of breath.
"I'm fine, I am always tripping over things, I'm amazed I am still alive!"
"That makes two of us," I whispered. I remembered the first time an old dear had lunged over my toolbox. I had rushed home and got public liability insurance the same day.
"Would you like a drink Mr Akentoff?" She asked beaming at me. I assumed she was smiling at her effort to get my name right. It was as close as most people got.

"I would love a drink, coffee with two sugars please." I should have asked for one sugar but it was too late! Subconsciously I needed two.

I let her shuffle off to her kitchen then gathered all the bits up off the floor and put them back into the toolbox before getting down to work on the sewing machine. I did not like the way she had said it went bang and immediately looked for an electrical fault. It was not long before I found the trouble, a burnt-out suppressor below the motor. As I was replacing the part she arrived with my coffee. Her hands were so shaky that the inside of the cup looked like a stormy day of the Channel. I quickly took the coffee before it was splashed all over me. It was time for a break, I had been working since before it was light and a rest was just what I needed.

"Been sewing long Mrs Gable?" I asked expecting to hear a good story.
"Oh do call me Molly, everyone does. No, I only started when I retired and I did not retire until I was 73, so I have only been sewing three years. I bet that has surprised you?" She added sipping from her tea.
"Yes, I expected you to tell me you had been sewing all your life," I laughed.
"My sisters sewed you see, so there was no need for me to as well, they did everything for me. I was the youngest of the four girls and spoilt rotten. They are all gone now, gone to a better place and I shall be joining them soon. But not before I have another cup of tea."
"Not too soon I hope Molly. You will owe me some money for fixing your machine, perhaps you had better write out the cheque now." I smiled back at her.
"You never know when your time is up, mind you there is no point in worrying I find worry is such a waste of energy," replied Molly. "But I always get everything tidy. At night I leave the house perfect and all clean. My clothes are all folded neatly on the chair and if God decided to take me in the night everything is ready. I sleep like a baby knowing everything is in order, you know the old saying, *a well-spent day brings happy sleep and a well-spent life brings happy death*. Well, it is very true."

"Molly if you do not mind me asking, how many cups of tea do you drink in a day? I could not help noticing that you have had three while I have been here."
"Well, I used to drink up to 25 cups a day but when I developed arthritis in my fingers my doctor made me cut down. I did cut right down to 15 cups a day but that was hard. Then I heard that my doctor had died so now I am back up to 25 again and love every drop."
"Good for you, maybe that is what keeps you going."

"Yes, that and the drop of port before bedtime I dare say." Molly replied.

I left Molly tidying up her bungalow and headed inland towards my next call at Slye's Farm. Thoughts of Molly with an empty glass of port by her bedside, happily sleeping with her arms crossed like an Egyptian mummy each night, waiting for the *afterlife*, made me smile. Some people have just got it all sussed out.

At the farm I had the wonderful pleasure of finding out the machine had a wiring fault behind the switch. As I reached around to see where the wires went into the switch, 240 volts shot up my arm and shook my body. I jumped up and yelped like a whipped dog, the lady of the house jumped as well. I was left examining my fingers and stretching my muscles to ease the shock that had suddenly decided to visit my body. And apologizing for the outburst of foul language that had slipped out of my mouth under the influence of the voltage. Besides some slight burn marks there was no damage. I had survived yet another attack and lived to tell the tale.

Funny thing is, you often feel quite good after a shock. I have had dozens in my life and never succumbed to one yet. It is not that I am clumsy, far from it, I am the opposite, even to the point of being paranoid, yet somehow my good old customers still trap me. The worst one I ever had was from a car with electronic ignition, the system was rated at 46,000 volts and I had a humdinger of a shock from a faulty ignition box. Still, all in the line of duty. I might get to the stage where I wear rubber gloves and thick rubber Wellington boots to all my customers, but not just yet.

Once I had found the fault on the switch I soon had her industrial 16k Singer purring along. That machine had been sewing for nearly a century and still looked as if it had more life left in it than I did. I left Slye's Farm with her two filthy farm dogs charging around the side of the farm buildings. They were too late! I had put my tools in the boot and slammed the driver's door before the first mutt got to me. I looked down at the dirty dogs and waved lovingly as they barked and snapped at me. Most farm dogs are well-trained beasts but this pair seemed to take some evil pleasure in scaring me to death.

My trip through the autumn countryside to my next call, at Laughton, was pure pleasure. The small country tracks, through Ripe to Laughton, that hardly a soul uses, were empty, save for a couple of riders on their horses enjoying the autumn air. As I rolled up one small road, no wider than a farm track, a peacock standing in the middle of the road stopped me. It surveyed me with disgust as I hooted at it. What on earth was a peacock doing parading in the middle of the road? It reluctantly moved off into the hedgerow so that I could pass, giving me *the eye* as I went by.

Late autumn was unfolding before me as I drove and beautiful scenes of pre-winter Sussex were everywhere. These late autumn days are filled with extremes. It can be cold in the morning and blazing hot by midday, dry one minute and pouring the next. I stopped down a small track to pick some ripe blackberries that were hanging temptingly over the road. The smell of the countryside with the fresh, cool, air was inspiring. I breathed in deeply, the exquisite aroma of sweet oak and hawthorn, of sloe berries and ripe corn. It mingled so perfectly with the smell of Mother earth.

I watched for a moment. All around, signs of the on-coming winter were there to see. I had not noticed the morning until now. A golden sun had slipped quietly over Sussex, as soft and gentle as a mother's kiss on a sleeping baby. Flocks of Canadian Geese were noisily heading, arrow-shaped, towards their winter feeding grounds. A gentle breeze ruffled the drying leaves in the hedgerows sounding like a babbling brook.

The South Downs had lost their green coat, with the grass now a dull-sand colour. The last few dandelion and cornflowers were still showing, in fast disappearing patches of blues and yellows, clutching to the sheltered spots on the Downland. Hedge sparrows were busy darting in and out of the hedgerows, feasting on the bountiful fruits that were spilling over the hedges, like over-filled fruit bowls. Daddy-long-legs were ponderously labouring over the brambles, like miniature alien invaders from a distant galaxy, reminiscent of those old movies. On the telephone wires hundreds of starlings were chatting away excitedly. They were gathering for the great journey that they do every autumn. They would soon be heading over the South Downs, across the sea for the coast of France and Spain on their long journey to Africa for the winter. With them would be their young ones, born in the eaves of country cottages and barn lofts only months before. They would be on a journey of a lifetime, across ancient lands and places, across seas and mountain ranges, across forests and deserts that I would never see. No wonder they were excited, who wouldn't be?

There is something so magical about standing in the middle of nowhere, listening and watching nature at work. It fills up places in the soul that ancient races knew all about and we have forgotten. It makes us complete. It is a cure for all the modern stresses of daily life. A tonic.

No matter how busy I get, if I can just escape for a few moments into the countryside and join with nature, she replenishes me and fills me with new energy. If I could bottle the feeling that a deep breath of Sussex countryside gives you, it would be the best selling tonic in the world. I could sell it as **Snake Bite Al's Cure-All**. Guaranteed to uplift a dying dog and make it run a mile.

"Can't be anything much," Mrs Gibb was saying as I looked into the top of her rusty old Alfa machine.
"How long has it been since you last used the machine?" I asked doubting that it had ever been used to sew.
"Last year I think, or maybe the year before that? I definitely sewed with it that year… I think," she replied looking vaguely at me. She obviously had no idea at all.
"It has a seized bearing and it is going to take some work to get it moving again," I told her, wondering if I was going to be able to repair the machine.
"Well I'll get the coffee on while you start work," she added.
"Sounds good to me," I smiled back.

Before long the rusty old machine had succumbed to my loving touch and was sewing away with the usual clunky noise that is so familiar to the Spanish Alfa machines.

I was just starting to pack away my tools when Mrs Gibb's 18-month-old daughter appeared in the doorway. A pretty little girl with blonde curls tumbling around her plump face. However it was not all sweetness and light. From her nose ran two huge lines of snot. She wobbled towards me in that funny way little kids walk with their nappies on, their huge oversized bums waggling like duck's backsides. She had a tissue in her hand and in slow motion she lifted the tissue and smeared the snot across her face. It was a failed attempt to wipe some of it away. She was grinning at me. I was horrified. I just knew what she was going to do next. She started toddling towards me, holding up the snot-smeared tissue, I backed away in horror, but there was nowhere to go.

I frantically waved her away. "No, no, not me, give it to your mum, Mrs Gibb!" I shouted, backing closer and closer into the corner of the room as the alien *snot creature* from planet *zog* moved ominously closer.

"Mrs Gibb," I called in desperation. "Your daughter has a little present for you."

By now I was trapped in the corner of the room. The little blonde devil was still grinning and thrusting the snot-rag up at me.

"Look, darling it's your mummy you want, not big fat me, I'm a monster, I eat little children like you for breakfast." My words had no effect, she just grinned even more and started to giggle. As she giggled, two more huge candlesticks of slime started to slide down her face.

"Please sweetie, just be a good little girl and run away," I said with no effect, I had no choice but to face the music.

Reluctantly I bent down and looked for a corner of the tissue that was not covered in a billion germs. Apprehensively I reached out with my thumb and forefinger and gently prised the tissue out of her tiny hand. She just stood there with the biggest smile you could imagine, her face slightly raised in anticipation. It suddenly dawned on me that not only did she want me to take the tissue, she wanted me to wipe her snot-ridden face as well!

This was a new game she had learnt and I could tell that she liked it. I braced myself, held my breath, swallowed and knelt down.

"There, there, that's better isn't it?" I said wiping her face. I folded the moist slimy tissue and wiped it again. Just when I had finished her mum appeared, saw what was happening and laughed.

"I see she has caught you then?"

"Yes, thanks for saving me, better late than never," I said holding up the tissue in disgust. "Got somewhere I can put this?"

"Drop it in the kitchen bin under the sink. She has had a terrible cold all week. You had also better wash your hands straight away or you will be coming down with one as well."

I straightened up and headed for the kitchen with the tissue extended out in front of me like a scientist with a virus sample.

"I am glad you managed to wipe it up, a lot of men would just have called for help," she added.

"Ah that's no problem, she didn't scare me," I said, passing her.

"Oh, she didn't hey, so why were you crammed into the far corner of the room then?"

"Ok, you got me. It was either leap over your daughter and run out of the room or take it like a man."

"You are all the same you men, one child with a cold and you are reduced to a wreck."

She had a good laugh at my expense and her daughter seemed to be enjoying all the fuss we were making over her. I washed up – no, I scrubbed up and finished packing my tools away. All the time, keeping a close eye out for another assault by the *bogey baby*. I waved to them both, standing in the doorway of their home and hit the road to my next customer.

"Ah, just what the doctor ordered." I said as Mrs Young brought in a lovely, hot cup of coffee and two digestive biscuits. I felt confident that I would only eat one biscuit and then stick to my waning diet. I had been working away for an hour on her 1963 Harris machine and it was still not responding.

"Perhaps I should not have left it in the shed." She said as she peered down over the machine that was stripped down and scattered all over her living room table.

"Yes, you are right. There are two things that kill sewing machines, one is dropping them and the other is rust. However, I see the light at the end of the tunnel with yours and I am sure she will be running as sweet as a nut in no time at all."

It had been a long morning and I needed a drink like a flower needed water. I was wilting fast. Ok, so I am a rather large flower, perhaps one of those Amazonian trifid monsters? Still, the coffee worked its magic and **both** digestive biscuits slipped down with equal ease, they would ensure that I would unfortunately sustain my ample waistline but were thoroughly enjoyed.

Before long the machine was up and running and the Land Rover was pointed towards Eastbourne for the next call at Cavendish School. I look after many schools in my area, some good, some not so good. Going into a school classroom is to me a real enjoyment, and a trip down memory lane.

I was in Mary's class, a well-organised and happy class that reflected her excellent ability to teach her pupils. Schools are all about the teachers. It is something that we so quickly forget. Endless governments try to change schools to suit their ideals. The lifeblood of a school can be judged by the morale of the teachers. If it is high, the school nearly always does well in all it tries to achieve. Lose the morale of the teachers and everyone suffers. It is like breaking up a winning team. In recent years I have seen so many teachers off school with different illnesses, nearly all of them are stress related.

Mary's class was busy with GCSE projects. One by one the children held their project up to the others to let them see how they were doing. I sat like a school kid, completely forgetting that I was supposed to be fixing machines and watched my childhood being repeated to a new generation.

I had a tricky job in front of me, an internal motor replacement on a Frister & Rossmann. I began silently working as the first drops of rain tapped against the windows and heavy gusts of wind made the trees shiver outside. The changeable autumn weather was with us. Inside I felt warm, bright and safe in my colourful classroom, as if it did not matter what the cruel world was doing outside the room. As if all life revolved around this one bright shiny room, full of hope and enthusiasm for the future.

The last time I was here it was a different matter. One of the new machines had gone wrong at the worst possible time, in the middle of an exam. I was just sitting down to lunch when the phone rang.

"Hello Alex, it's Mary here, Cavendish School. We have a crisis! One of the machines has broken half way through the exam. I have got no spare machines as all the others are being used."
"Mary," I interrupted, "breathe or you are going to pass out."
"I'm sorry, but I am all wound up! Can you help? You must help now! Can you come now, right now?"
"Mary, I am on my way."

I had jumped into the Land Rover and bolted down the road, within 10 minutes I was at the front entrance of the school. Mary was waiting at reception.

"No time to sign in and get your badge, just follow me." Mary said, grabbing my arm and almost lifting me along the school corridor.

I was marched straight passed all of the **Do not disturb** and **Examination in progress** signs to the classroom. There, on a bench was the sewing machine, jammed with the cloth still tight in the needle plate. Sitting by the side was a girl with tears in her eyes. They were tears of frustration and panic, she had 45 minutes left to finish her piece of work and the clock was ticking. I worked like a demon and before long the machine was up and running. I had saved the day, for one pupil anyway. I later learnt that she had passed her GCSE with an A+, the highest possible mark in the exam.

After a successful motor transplant on the Frister, I packed my tools away, and bade farewell to Mary. She called me a *star*. It is so nice to please people I thought to myself as I left the building feeling almost heroic – well, as close as I get to it in my job – I made my way back to the car. I walked slowly along the corridors like a parent on parent's evening, looking at all the work and pictures posted along the corridor walls.

My job leads me into many places, from car factories to hospitals, which all have their points of interest. I am the fly on the wall watching daily life go round while not really being part of it. I drift from one call to another, momentarily touching down onto someone's life then disappearing again. I often stop in the factories and enjoy the tea breaks when they all get together and chat about nothing of importance. The Christmas dance or what's on at the cinema. That is probably the one thing I miss most about the loss of my families business. Being part of a team.

Small businesses run as teams, they have great trouble even if one person is off sick. A well-run business, whether it is a school, a laundry, a hotel or hospital, is rarely top-heavy with extra staff, they have just enough. Each person is a cog in an engine. If one cog fails the whole engine or rather business, suffers.

I like to feel that I add my little effort to the scheme of things, keeping the wheels of industry turning, in homes and businesses all along my corner of the world.

I drove out of the school car park and headed home. Time indeed for a nice cuppa and yet another exhilarating bowl of rabbit food. I could never have imagined the endless ways in which lettuce and vegetables could be prepared but still taste the same!

The Laughton Village Stores, a delightful store that just oozes character. You can do everything here from post a letter to America, pick up a gas bottle for your barbecue or simply buy an ice cream.

Out in the Cold

This machine has been converted from sewing buttons onto garments into one sewing lead-filled rope onto fishing nets. I often find one minute I am working in an old shed like this one, the next, a country house. Here I am performing my usual open-heart surgery on the internal workings of the machine.

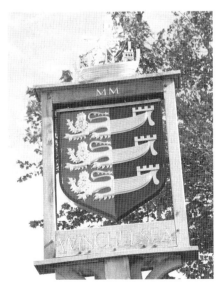

All the towns and villages have these signs, but the Winchelsea sign is the best I have seen.

The 12th Century St. Mary's in Rye, with its immortal words above the clock tower. "For our time is a very shadow that passeth away."

OINK OINK

The sun was breaking over the South Downs with orange light bursting through the heavy broken cloud heaving great beams of radiance into the fading darkness. Skeins of wild geese were lifting from the valley, their under-bodies caught in the early morning glow. The majestic birds were noisily calling to each other as they flew over me in their typical V-formation, like a bomber squadron on a dawn mission. Autumn leaves were silently falling and a cool wind was rushing up the dark vale. I stood for a moment by the side of my Land Rover, watching in silent awe as the spectacle unfolded before me. Early morning had brought a temporary lull in the autumn storms that had been raging over East Sussex. The autumn equinox was almost upon us and England's most beautiful month was unfolding before me. Like a great aunt in a wonderful evening gown, she was out to impress all that care to look. And for a few seconds in the early dawn she was young again.

Tim, the Border collie, was staring at me wondering what I was up to, his head jammed enthusiastically out of the cat flap. He looked so silly as he barked to his owner at my approach. His head was framed in grey plastic, like a 3D moving image. He barked again while he stared at my every move with his one, big blue eye and the other green eye. There was no need to knock now that I had been announced. Tim disappeared to fetch someone and I waited by the door.

I saw a small blue and grey shape struggling with the lock. She took ages and tried the handle, then tried again. The third time the door slowly opened and a grinning little girl in her new, school uniform proudly announced, "It's my first day at school today, I am going to learn how to spell and do maffs."

"Well, you make sure to listen to your teacher really well, so that you can tell your mum all about it later," I answered as I followed her into her living room. Her mum was on the phone and waved me over to her industrial machine in the corner.

"Sorry about that, you know what it is like, everything always happens at once," she said, hanging up the phone and walking across the room to clear some half-made curtains off the machine.

"It's amazing you know. When I first called on you, your daughter was not even born and now she is off to school! Time flies, doesn't it?"

"Best not think about it really. Just enjoy it while we are here," Vicky replied.

I soon got down to work on the industrial machine and within the hour it was running up a row of stitches like its old self.

As I left, Vicky was loading her little girl into the back of their car for their very first trip to school. Tim whined pathetically, with his head, once again, jammed through the cat flap. Poor thing, everybody was leaving home except him.

The huge winds that had erupted with the autumn storms were back, throwing conkers all over the roads from the horse chestnut trees, scattering them like mini hand grenades. Leaves in every conceivable shade of autumn had been prised away from their branches and lay along the sides of the road. There were the yellow from elm and ash, the brown chestnut and deep aubergine of the copper beech, the gold of the oak and pale sycamore, reds and gold, green and crimson, like discarded sweet wrappers in a school playground. Twigs were strewn everywhere, they had yielded to the unrelenting wind howling through their branches and in one last snap, fell and howled no more. The warm breeze was losing its battle with the approaching cold winter. However, it was putting up a valiant fight along the way. As I drove, the trees and bushes twisted and turned in an airy turmoil, like possessed dancers on a dance floor. I was warm and dry inside my car watching the panoramic cinema performance outside.

I pulled up to the house of my next customer, on a back road to Battle. I was calling at *Green Man Cottage* to service an old Pfaff treadle machine. I expected an old dear to open the warped oak door. Instead, a young energetic woman in her early thirties greeted me. She looked like one of the old *land girls* from the war era. She was wearing denim jeans, turned up to her calves and a bright, blue-checked, gingham blouse with the sleeves pulled up to her elbows. Her blonde hair was tied back behind her head with a blue scarf.

"Hello, I have come to fix your machine," I announced in my most professional and upbeat tone.

"Ah, do come in. I have been expecting you, it is all ready in the hall," she said with a bright smile.

She led me into her beautiful home that had low-slung oak beams on ceilings no more than six feet high. There was a musty, but pleasant, smell that only ancient homes acquire after centuries of use. I need not have ducked but subconsciously did so anyway as I walked behind her to the machine.

"It is my mother's machine, she bought it new in 1952. She did not want anything electric as they kept having power cuts in the 1950s and they drove her mad. So she had the treadle, power-cut-proof, you see. I am afraid I have let it get into rather a bad way over the last few years. That's why I phoned you. Time, I thought, for a nice service."

"Yes indeed," I replied looking at the machine and rocking the hand wheel. "There is nothing like a good clean and oil to get these old machines running again."

"Oh, and after you have finished, could you show me how to use the machine as I have never sewn with it?"

"No problem," I answered, it won't take long. "I shall give you a shout when I am all done."

"Right, I am just in the other room finishing some work. I will be putting the kettle on shortly, would you like a drink?"

"Love one," I replied, "coffee with two sugars please."

Oops, once again I had let two sugars slip out. If my diet was to have a chance of succeeding I must cut back… Anyway it was too late now and the thought of a nice sweet coffee sounded really appealing. She toddled off into the other room and started banging away at something. It sounded like she was trying to knock the house down. No sooner had the banging stopped, when a sander started and that went on for a few more minutes, then all went quiet.

The lovely mellow sound of the grandfather long-case clock in the hall drifted into the silence. Its slow, perfect, pendulum ticking away. There is always something so nice about the silence after loud noise. Shortly after, my *land girl* appeared with a hot cup of coffee. My eyes lit up as I saw two chocolate biscuits nudged around the edge of the saucer. I smiled as I took the drink and bickies – well, I hadn't asked for the biscuits and it would have been rude to refuse them. Anyway, food given as a gift contains **no** calories, or so I'm told!

"I am decorating the spare room." She announced with a real sense of pride in her voice. "I have never done anything like it before. Normally my husband does it but he is too busy at the moment, so I have taken on the task – and love it."

"I can see," I said, noting that she was covered, from head to toe, in plaster and dust. I sipped my coffee while she showed me around her handiwork. It looked good. She obviously had the knack for decorating. All the wood had been stripped and all the little filled holes in the walls had been smoothed away. All in all a very professional job.

"Well, if it looks as good as this when it is finished I think your husband will be really pleased with it. Is that what the sewing machine is for, new curtains?"
"Got it in one," she smiled.

We spent the next half-an-hour going through all the tricky little procedures she had to follow when using her treadle. I left her bombing along on a test piece of fabric. I wish I had a camera to hand. She looked as if she was from a different time, what she was wearing suited the old house and sewing machine perfectly. They looked like a matched set from a long-forgotten past.

I had not thought about the awful weather outside while fixing the machine. I stood in the doorway looking out at the storm that was still raging. I shrugged my shoulders. There was nothing for it but to run to the car. As I ran, sheets of rain were flying along, almost horizontally instead of downward. The rain tore and lashed at my face. It was almost impossible to see where I was going. I rushed, head bowed, to the car. Thick, thunderous, clouds in deep, rumbling greys were throwing down their wrath upon the drenched soil as they lumbered across the Sussex skyline. They were so low and ponderous they looked like you could reach out and touch them. I pulled the car door open and leapt in then wrenched it closed as fast as I could. I heaved a sigh of relief and sat for a moment gathering my breath while the car rocked in the wind.

The roads were awash as the Land Rover *puddle-hopped* its way down to my next customer, a few miles the other side of Battle. He was an old tailor that had kept his last machine when he retired. It was a Singer 66K that had seen hard times. The enamel on the bed of the machine had worn away into a semi-circle from endless years of hard work.

"Would not be without the old girl," he piped up as I started to remove the side plate. "Cost me a months wages back in '49," he threw in. "Wounded in the war, you see, and the machine, well, sewing was the only job I could do after – tailoring that is."

Harry went on to tell me all about being shot on the beaches of Normandy, dragged back to an emergency field hospital and shipped home within days.

"All happened so fast, my feet didn't touch the ground, the war was over for me in two days. Mind you, left me with a limp for life. Still, can't complain, many of my mates never made it home for supper. I made it back, but you know what they say, *the devil looks after his own.*"

Harry talked non-stop at the speed of light. He didn't breathe; he didn't even offer me a drink. Couldn't do that. It would stop him from talking to me. It became obvious that I was there to hear his life story. Well, his condensed one-hour, visitor version of it. As I left he was still spilling out words like a food-mixer with the lid off. He did make me laugh! Trouble is, when I laugh, I forget, so the result was that, even though Harry was so interesting, most of his verbal onslaught was lost. Thrown to the ether and gone forever. I could no more remember his stories than grab a word out of the air. I shall just have to pay him another visit and get him to relax somehow, then I could soak up his life.

My next call was a sad one, a last visit to The College, in Priory Road, Hastings. It was being closed down after a century of teaching. As I walked along the silent building I bumped into the caretaker who was cleaning up.

"Thirty years I have been doing this job and even though they are closing it down, I can't help myself, got to keep it all *spik 'n' span*," he said in a sad resigned voice. His head seemed to be more drooped than normal. Maybe it was just my imagination, but every inch of his body seemed to be oozing sadness.

I could not help but sympathise with him. I had called on the college many times over the years to look after their machines. Now they were to be taken to separate places, all split up. It was the end of an era.

As I left the old redbrick Edwardian building, I knew I would never return. There would be no more kids running up the stairs shouting with excitement, no more classrooms full of students learning how to run the world. Still, the world turns and, if we are part of it, we have no choice but to turn with it.

I drove by the last piece of open ground between St Leonards and Bexhill. It was another worrying sight. A notice-board had been placed for all to see, **LAND SOLD**. Drainage pipes were being laid where wild field mice once ran and marsh reeds swayed in the breeze. Where the circus would come to visit every year to entertain the wide-eyed and excited children.

Typical council! The one, last, open space still had to be sold off for some sort of development. They could not even keep one, little field. One day there will be one big sprawling mass of houses all along, from Little Common to Cooden, Bexhill, St Leonards and to Hastings. Only after that, will the soft green Sussex landscape open once again. Allowing the sweeping views over the beautiful countryside.

Still, there are two problems with the land that any developer is going to have trouble with. Firstly it is very boggy and will be difficult to build on and secondly the traffic is so bad along that road that, whoever is going to live on a new estate in that location is going to have a hard job pulling out of their drive. They will have to leave half-an-hour early each day just to get out of the end of their road.

By late morning I was having hunger-pangs again. I arrived at my last customer before lunch and the thought of another awful salad, back home, was none too appealing. It is amazing how you can come to hate something with such venom. I now felt that way about *iceburg* lettuce! The coffee and biscuits I had earlier in the morning had been long forgotten by my stomach.

Pearl was a lovely old girl, my sort of perfect customer. She first visited Bexhill-on-Sea in 1937. Her father was a concert pianist and would spend the summer season playing at the impressive, *art deco*, De La Warr Pavilion, on Bexhill seafront. The pavilion is, at the moment, in a poor state of repair. However there is a light at the end of the tunnel and a huge grant is in the offing to completely restore the wonderful addition to Bexhill seafront to its former 1930's glory.

I look after the sewing machine at The De La Warr. It is always a pleasure to see the theatre all quiet, with a sleeping stage behind the velvet curtains. Everything ready as if frozen in time, just waiting. Waiting for the curtains to slowly open. Waiting for the spotlight to burst into life and swing down onto the stage. Waiting for the performer, caught in the ball of brilliant light, to announce the show. Waiting for the audience to explode with applause at the start of the evening's entertainment. Yes, a sleeping stage is something to behold.

The De La Warr Pavilion has been described as one of the world's first and finest examples of *modernist architecture*. This may be a slight exaggeration but it is a fine building. The Ninth Earl De La Warr held an international competition to build a place of entertainment on the empty Bexhill seafront to entertain Bexhill's visitors. The winner was a German architect, Erich Mendelsohn. His free lines and sweeping curves fitted in perfectly with the curving beachfront and the open spirit of the sea. To make his design possible he had to use innovative welded steel frames and I believe that it was one of the first buildings in England to use such building techniques in its construction. Of course, today we think nothing of these building methods but in 1934 it was revolutionary. The result is an open, sweeping building with an air of grace and elegance.

While Pearl's father played at the theatre, Pearl would sit and watch or, sometimes play with her new friends that she would meet on the beach. It was a lovely childhood in the sweet, innocent, safety of the pre-war era. When Pearl married, the happy couple moved down to Bexhill permanently. Her husband was a cabinet maker and, as his name was Shilling, in every piece of furniture he ever made he would place a shilling into the wood. His trademark. So, if you ever find a cabinet with an Old-English shilling stuck in it, well, now you know why.

As I entered her house I was greeted by a marvellous smell. I was enticed, no entranced, like one of the little kids of an old Bisto advert. I closed my eyes and breathed in the most wonderful smell. Pearl was in the middle of making Bliney – Russian pancakes. It was her first attempt and they smelled simply irresistible. I was wet and hungry. The warm house, with the aroma of fresh pancakes, was so welcoming and I love pancakes… who doesn't? It was as enticing as an oasis in the desert to a lost Bedouin.

With my usual luck I had called at the perfect time. Pearl asked me to check the pancakes for taste and lightness. I did not need much persuading. I subconsciously thought I would limit myself to just one. So as not to ruin my diet!

"Perfect Bliney," I reported, after the first pancake had disappeared down my throat with delight. "As light as air and sweet as nectar," I added.

Pearl was obviously overwhelmed at my enthusiastic description and quickly cooked me another. Good plan, I thought, wondering how I could next describe her pancakes to encourage her to feed me all afternoon.

All thoughts of diets were flung to the four winds. If anyone should know about Bliney, it is me. At our family home, when I was a kid, pancakes were a favourite breakfast meal, what with my Dad being Russian an' all. Pearl was in heaven cooking away. I was close behind, stuffing my face.

Outside the storm was still raging. Her patio doors were being buffeted by the gale, the doors were shaking as if the invisible man was trying to get in. Tough luck mate, I thought, no room in here and no spare pancakes either Buster!

After my sixth pancake I felt like a bloated sow in a cabbage patch. I decided I had better waddle off to fix her machine before I collapsed headfirst into the next pancake. Dying with a delighted smile on my face. I patted my belly with much pleasure as I started work. *What a meal*, I thought, now all I needed was a few hour's kip. Mind you, I don't expect Pearl would be too pleased if she found me asleep on her sofa for the afternoon.

Instead, I reluctantly went to work and fixed her Janome machine while she cleaned up. Within the hour her machine had been serviced and set. As I was leaving I could not help notice a rather large wooden cudgel behind her front door. It was a whopper. The sort that *Bill Sykes* from *Oliver Twist* would carry around the streets of London, with his dog hot on his heels.

"What on earth is that for?" I asked.

"Oh that's for the vicar at St Mary's, down the road," she smiled with a wicked grin. "He called me an *old dolly* once. So, when he next calls, collecting for the church steeple or some other good deed, I am going to give him a good whack with it. You know, stroke the back of his head with a bit of tender-loving care. You see I am a converted Anglo-Catholic and he is from a lower order, so I need to keep him in line."

I hoped she was joking, but you can never be sure with some of my customers. I could just imagine the court case. Exhibit 'A' being the cudgel. What a dilemma! I could always appear as a character witness. The last thing that I wanted was my *Bliney* specialist locked up in the clink.

We parted company, with Pearl holding the wooden cudgel and practising her swing, while I was still rubbing my contented, overfed, belly. As I left I was looking forward to a return visit in the future. Secretly hoping that her machine would not sew perfectly for too many years. Because, boy, those pancakes were good!

I drove homeward along the marsh road with that special feeling that only comes from great food. Even on such a dull and wet day I could see the outline of the beautiful Downs in the distance, with the dip just above my home. I knew the miles would soon be covered back to my door.

I passed by Wallers Haven, the lovely river where the large pike would be on the feed for their winter rations. Many a pike had fallen to my bait, on that river, over the years. I drove by the old Pevensey post office looking lost and neglected since its closure and the Old Pevensey court house, where many a drunk had spent the night after becoming inebriated at The Smugglers Inn. Just along a smidgen is the Old Mint House where coinage was struck and is now a fabulous antique store, which I often visit. Upstairs, the owner has several rare sewing machines but he never sells them, I know I have tried several times to get them.

I went by the great gate of Pevensey Castle where William the Conqueror landed on September 28th 1066. The castle had been up for centuries before he made his temporary camp there. By the time he arrived, the old Roman fort had become little more than a Saxon shore fort. Today the castle is just a reminder of our mixed ancestry and violent past. I drove on, around the hairpin bends that follow the castle walls.

Opposite the castle, lies the *Tudor Priory Court Hotel*. Light from inside was floating softly, through the diamond-leaded windows. It looked so inviting on such a stormy day. I passed the haunted cottage in Westham High Street. It is next to the first Norman church ever built on English soil. The church was built in 1080 AD, less than 14 years after the Norman Conquest. It shows how much the French had secured their domination of England. Square-spired Norman churches are a common feature dotted around our English landscape. Amazingly, South East England has the highest concentration of medieval churches in the entire world. Now, I bet that was a fact you just could not live without!

I joined in with the busy Langney traffic, flowing towards the Stone Cross Windmill. It stands proud in the distance. From the Westham end of Langney, the windmill looks much as it must have done for over a century. Built on a slight hill to harness the wild wind that rushes through the valley from the sea. Rolling fields, a few houses and farms would have surrounded the mill. Now it is a very different matter. New housing estates are creeping right up to her white skirts. She seems completely out of place, lost in the new Eastbourne suburbs.

As I got home, Yana greeted me. "That large barge carrying thousands of tons of granite for the sea defences has capsized just off Langney Point. There was no one on board. It looks like a giant submarine. It has just been on the T.V. Would you like a bite to eat? You must be famished," she carried on as I sat down, "I have prepared a **lovely salad** for you."
"Oh, never mind, I am not that hungry," I replied.
She was suspicious in an instant! "Come on then! Who has been feeding you and what was it this time?" She asked with her usual, *I give up with him* voice.

She knew straight away that I had managed to winkle some food out from some unsuspecting customer on my rounds. Under her sustained pressure

I had to recount my delightful meal of the **three** wonderful Russian pancakes. Well, no one could eat six – could they?
Hey! They would have to be a right pig, **oink, oink**.

The front façade of the superb De La Warr Pavilion on Bexhill seafront. The winner of a competition held in 1934 to find the perfect Building for Bexhill, It stands today as an early example of modernistic architecture

WINTER DRAWS IN

"You cannot be serious!" I said to the lady as I looked on in horror at the mangled old industrial Singer 96K in her open barn. "You want me to fix this, here, today, in this weather?"

"Well, if you could just give it the once over that would be nice," the lady said in her most pleasant *I gave you an order, now follow it tone.*

"This is going to need more than a once over. I can see half-a-dozen bits missing and God only knows how bad it is underneath!"

"Well, I have heard that you are the man when it comes to industrial machines, I am sure you can work wonders. I'll just pop off and fetch you a coffee."

With that she disappeared up the yard towards her cottage, not giving me a chance to answer. I knew I was wasting my time trying to say anything. She wanted the machine fixed and was not taking **no** for an answer.

It was an awful day. The first really cold day of the winter. Summer was just a distant memory and autumn had left with a resigned sigh. Winter was relentlessly clawing back East Sussex for the dark months ahead. Freezing winds were howling down from the Scottish Highlands bringing snow flurries with them.

What was I to do? I was standing in the yard, beside an open barn, on the side of a hill, shivering. This is when the true spirit of the self-employed cuts in. An empty pocket at the beginning of the day is a powerful motivator.

Out in the field a bay mare looked over at me with a longing in her eyes for a nice warm rug to keep the chilled wind off. I decided I would just have to do my best and get down to work. I moved my trusty Land Rover right up to the mouth of the barn and parked it as close as I could to the machine. At least some of the warmth from the engine would help a little. I pulled on my woolly hat and waterproof overcoat that hides under the car seat for most of the year and got down to work.

What a change! I thought. My previous call had been at a lovely semi in Uckfield, with central-heating and double-glazing. Now I was cowering in an open barn with my toes curling up in my shoes. After a few, frantic minutes and a number of replacement parts the machine started to look more like a sewing machine than an item of scrap. The woman appeared with a welcome mug of coffee. She hurried across the yard, her head bowed against the wind with her scarf trailing. A small head of steam was rolling off the top of the mug like the funnel of a steam train. It was a welcome sight and I grasped it with both hands, blowing down into the steaming drink and warming my hands on the mug.

"She is going to come up all right," I shouted to the woman as she ran back to the safety and comfort of the house.

"Good, good, I knew you could do it," she replied, not slowing down or looking back but raising an arm, as if in approval.

With shaking hands and freezing toes, I carried on the unenviable task of bringing the old machine back into working order. As I was working, I kept hearing strange sounds that hardly rose above the noise of the wind. Each time I heard them I stopped and looked around the cold open barn but I could see nothing. There it was again, 'tu-whit tu-whoo' I straightened up from where I was crouched over the machine and moved more into the barn. I removed my woolly hat and stared up into the dark eaves. In the dim pale light, I could just make out two dull domed shapes up on a wooden beam. As my eyes became accustomed to the lack of light, the shapes turned into two beautiful Tawny Owls. They sat there motionless, staring with dark eyes straight at me. They were much darker than I had thought they were supposed to be, they were the colour of chestnut leaves in the autumn, a reddish-brown. I watched in quiet admiration for a few moments as they huddled together all fluffed up against the cold. The cold also reminded me that I had work to do.

I got back down to work with my companions occasionally *cooing* to each other while watching my every move. I flicked the switch to turn on the motor of the industrial machine. The motor grunted into life winding up its speed and rattling the stand. The two reclusive onlookers had had enough, the startled owls shot out of the barn screeching into the chill wind as they went. I watched as they became no more than dark specks in the distance, flying North into the snowy dimness. *Well*, I thought *that's not a sight you see every day*.

I finished off the industrial and left it fully threaded with nice thick thread for the horse blanket and packed all my tools back into the car. I wrote out the bill in the car, with the engine rumbling away and the heater on full blast. I thought about adding a few quid for having to freeze my butt off but the idea of the horse prancing around with a nice thick, waxed, horse blanket and a big horsy grin made me charge my usual amount. Of course, the perfectly timed cup of coffee was also a big plus in the customers favour.

I was glad to leave the call and head off towards Gun Hill. I was going to an old customer of mine with a nice, warm cottage. Mill View Cottage was well over 400 years old and, for some reason, it had escaped being a listed building. I suppose no planning officer had noticed it tucked away down the little country lane. It meant the owners could install all the latest features, like double-glazing and cavity-wall insulation without the council persecuting them. In buildings of this age you have to watch each step you take or you get a whack on the head from an unwelcome oak beam. I was still shivering inside from my previous encounter but soon warmed up with some good company and more hot drinks.

"Any ghosts living here Nelly?" I asked hopefully. Nothing better than a good ghost story to liven up the morning and these old cottages usually have a story or two hidden in their old walls.
"No I am afraid not. We have been here 30 years and not so much as a whisper."
"Well, you can't have everything can you?" I replied a bit disappointed.
"Oh, I could tell you about our neighbour's mother's funeral last week, that was quite a bash!"
"That's OK," I replied.

Not quite the same thing really I thought. Mind you, some of these locals have a fair old do when they *fall off their twig*. They almost have more fun when they are dead than when they were still breathing!

I met one old lady who kept her husband on the table for three days before she let the funeral directors cart him off to the cemetery.
"Just to say her goodbyes properly," she told me.

My last call of the morning was up a long old track, off the Burwash Road. The old couple had lived without all the modern conveniences for over a quarter of a century and were the most self-sufficient people I had ever met. They kept an old Singer shuttle machine handy for repairs. The last time I had called, it was late summer with the cornfields high and ripe, shimmering in the autumn sunlight. Today was a little different, the cold wind was sweeping over the bare farmland that had been tilled and turned ready for the spring crops. The soil lay barren and open to the elements waiting for the warm spring sunshine that was a long way off.

When I arrived, Harry was up a metal structure that looked like a small version of the Eiffel Tower.

"Blasted generator has packed up again," he shouted down to me as I got out of the car. "Typical! Could not have broken down on a nice day could it, *poxy* thing!"
"Need a hand Harry?" I shouted up to him through the biting wind, hoping that he did not. Luckily he was just about finished and I grabbed some of his tools as he stumbled down the last rung of his ladder. The old lad was seventy, if a day, and yet here he was out in all weathers. I watched as he walked over to the big red switch just above a pile of batteries in an outbuilding.
"Here goes nothing," he shouted and flung the switch over. A small bulb swinging above his head started to glimmer. The big smile that stretched across Harry's face meant that all was well. We headed inside, out of the elements.

At the old farmhouse, the kitchen Aga welcomed us with a characteristic rich smoky aroma that only those old wood-burning stoves have. I put my toolbox down as Harry's wife pulled his coat off him and hung it over the stove. She busily buzzed around him like an old queen bee, fussing over him and drying his hair with a towel. Harry just looked at me with his ruddy face and gave me a cheeky smile. His big red cheeks glowing with satisfaction at the pampering he was receiving. He peered outside up to the top of the mast where the little wind generator was spinning like a top.

"We should get some good juice out of her today dear, I think you will be able to watch both soaps tonight if the wind keeps up!"

I looked on in quiet admiration. The old couple had managed without any running water or electricity for decades. Water was pumped up from the well into a large container strapped up a tree near the cottage. It supplied all their needs. Electricity came and went with the wind. On a good day they got two hours of juice at night. They live today much as many must have once and they relished every second of it. In fact, Harry once told me, they were comfortable on their state pension. Probably the only old couple in Britain who could have said that. They had no bills from the Water Board or Electricity company, no gas or heating to pay for, just their food and clothing.

How did they do it? I wondered. But sitting in their kitchen watching the two of them together the answer was easy to see. They were deeply in love, every movement, every action, came from a lifetime of devotion to each other. They were a pleasure to watch and brought a quiet smile to my face as I fixed the sewing machine.

I never charged the couple much, they never said anything about it. But the charge to them has stayed the same in all the years I have called on them. The fault with the machine was usually a simple one anyway. I often wonder if they realise that I hardly covered my fuel costs. But, I tell you this, I would go there for free, any day, just to see the look on their faces as they fuss around each other. It is a look of true love, something that only grows after years of being together. It is a look that many a philosopher has pondered over and tried to grasp. In truth, no words could ever explain the devotion of this old couple who live outside the normal confines of life, in their own little cottage, down a track in the middle of nowhere.

In quiet moments, I often think about them, miles away from anywhere, happy in their isolation. I wonder what they are doing. It is easy to imagine the couple cuddled up together in front of a roaring fire, watching Coronation Street flickering away on their old black and white television hoping that *poxy* wind generator keeps spinning outside.

The Sussex Sheep are a hardy breed and well suited to the open rugged downland. In winter the wind can pour over the exposed South Downs like liquid ice.

The Smugglers at Pevensey. Many pubs bear this name now and you often wonder about the illegal dealings that went on for centuries.

The first Norman church built on British soil at Pevensey. Locals say several ghosts inhabit the area around the church and nearby castle.

EARLY DIP

Sunrise was still nearly an hour away as I scraped the frozen windscreen of the Land Rover. The heavy diesel engine spluttered reluctantly into life, sounding like a London taxi. I headed eastward towards Hastings and my first call of the morning at Rosemary's Sewing Basket in Queens Road. Rosemary's was one of those lovely shops that sold just about everything to do with sewing. Rosemary had learnt from her early years on the markets, exactly what her customers wanted.

As I drove, the soft silvery silence of the star bright night slipped quietly into dawn. The sky lifted to a quiet blue and the stars faded. I could just make out the silhouettes of sheep grazing in the cold fields along the marsh road they were almost lost to the eye, half hidden in a pale mist. The shortest day of the year was almost upon us. The sun would edge her way into our world, chasing the darkness away a second or two before 8 am and then disappear before 4 pm in the early afternoon. These sharp winter days are short but oh so sweet when the weather is right.

Within an hour the clear pallid horizon over the sea had changed to a deep orange like the rising flames of a grand fire. I had arrived at Rosemary's slightly early and made my way around the fishermen's huts at the end of Hastings seafront. I was on a mission to get a beautiful dawn picture. I parked around the back of the net-drying huts and walked along the beach, every footstep making that unique crunching, gravelly, sound of footsteps on pebbles. I went by fishing boats that lay, strewn across the beach, leaning into the pebbles like beached whales. They looked like they had been randomly tossed onto the beach by a huge wave.

A few of the early fishermen were tinkering around, getting ready to launch their boats at the high tide that was fast approaching. I carefully picked my way around their nets and lobster pots, that were littered over the beach, and made my way down to the seashore. I was aware that the fisherman were watching the *stranger in their midst*. While they were looking I did not want to trip on their precious nets and make an idiot of myself. The sun was just a few seconds away from its majestic entrance into this cold, sharp, winter's day. Seagulls called to each other as they floated above me, searching amongst the fishermen's boats for any scraps.

I was ready – in the perfect spot – at the perfect time. The wind was pouring over the leaden sea like liquid glass, whisking the salty spray from the tops of the dark waves – akin to smoke from a chimney in a timeless scene. Grains of sand were biting at my ankles trying to find a way in to eat at my flesh and chill my bones. Little by little the sun peeked above the distant horizon, silent and smooth. The unstoppable, giant star was bringing dawn to England. Rays of orange and yellow light skipped over the tips of the waves, streaking towards the coast as another night-time was taking its leave.

I was poised, camera in hand, on the edge of the land to capture the perfect moment forever. Crouching down I found I could just get the ridges of the waves with the sun behind. It was going to be a real beauty of a picture!

I took the perfect shot with, one large wave rolling towards the coast, the tip of the wave being blown away in light spray and the giant, orange, orb lifting majestically behind. It was a cracker!

What I had failed to grasp was that the wave I had just photographed was coming my way! I was totally absorbed in the moment when a freezing rush of saltwater hit me on its way up the shingle. In a second I was soaked from the knees downward. I leapt backwards in shocked surprise but I was way too late! My shoes filled with tiny bits of grit and freezing water as the foamy wave clawed around my feet and slipped back into the sea. I stumbled up the beach shaking my legs like a wet dog.

"Now, I know you didn't want to do that!" came the loud booming voice from one of the fishermen. They were having hysterics further up the beach, laughing at my unwanted dip in the sea. I looked up at them and wondered how I could get by them without the humiliating barrage of abuse that I was bound to suffer from them. I just laughed back and waved with a face turning the same colour as the sun. I could see the funny side even though I was now soaking wet and freezing.

I ran as fast as I could on the gravel that was like quicksand on the slopes and got back to the car with the minimum of verbal from the fishermen. I stripped off my shoes and wrung out my socks. Then I shook as much shingle as I could out of them. With the car heater blowing full blast I tried, in vain, to warm my freezing toes and flick out more shingle from between my delicate little pinkies. I sat there freezing, laughing and wondering if the picture was worth it, all at the same time.

At Rosemary's, her two collie dogs sniffed inquiringly around my feet at the strange, salty, smell. You could not see that my legs were wet as I was wearing dark trousers and black shoes. I just squelched a bit as I walked. Still, I had no option but to get down to work. Luckily, I found a box of tissues and stuffed several of them down each shoe to try and get some of the damp out.

Throughout the morning no one noticed that I was damp from the knee down. Well, if they did, they did not say anything. You could just imagine someone calling on you to repair your sewing machine and noticing that they were soaked. How strange! Who could have guessed what I had been up to? Still, my rounds went perfectly and call after call were sorted as I worked my way back towards Eastbourne.

"Hang on a mo," said Sid, examining his old, army watch cocked up to the light in the centre of the dark room, "you are in for our late morning show."

No sooner had he finished than a flock of jackdaws descended upon his balcony. I was in the top flat of the pleasant Church Bailey homes just over the Westham railway lines and I was in for a surprise. It was like watching an old Hitchcock horror movie. The splendid sunrise over a clear sky had turned into the more usual drab winter's day, full of drizzle and heavy clouds in shades of deepening grey. The black sky was suddenly filled with squawking jackdaws flapping out of heavens, twisting and turning, descending like a flock of carrion-eaters onto a dying beast. They squabbled and pecked at each other, banging against the windows in their haste, grabbing the crusts of bread that Sid puts out for them each day.

"They arrive at 11:45 sharp every day and demolish the bread in a matter of seconds, then disappear as quickly as they arrive," he said, watching them with great satisfaction.

It was an eerie sight on such a bleak morning.

As Sid had said, they quickly cleared up the scraps from the balcony then flapped away, squawking as they went. Disappearing into the dull day as quickly as they had arrived. It suddenly reminded me of a time I had long forgotten. I find memories are often jogged by sights, sounds and smells.

I had been aimlessly floating down the Nile with the family on one of our adventures when I had an unnerving encounter.

It was early morning, I was half-asleep in bed when there came a tap on the window. I became vaguely aware of it, but did not respond. Perhaps I had misheard? The side of the vessel was flat, there were no balconies, no one could be there. Just the beautiful, ageless, Nile gliding past. But then it came again, as clear as day. Tap. Tap. Now I was jumpy! I gingerly got out of bed and crept to the heavily lined curtains. As I reached towards them, it came again. Tap. Tap. Tap. I jumped back! My mind racing in an early-morning haze of semi-consciousness. Once more I crept forward, I looked around to see Yana still fast asleep. I hesitated for a moment, then, bravely drew back the curtains.

Gripping the safety rail was a huge Nile Raven! I stepped back in shock, trying to focus in the glare of the brilliant morning light. The largest, most evil-looking raven I had ever seen stared, with one terrifying beady-eye, straight into my soul. My God! It has come to curse me – a foreigner in its land – I was going to be eaten by Ravens and sacred Scarab beetles for travelling the holy river without consent from the river gods.

I had been duly summoned for punishment. I froze in wide-eyed horror as it opened its shiny black beak, this was it – *the end*. The curse of a thousand infidels was about to be unleashed!

Instead, the raven picked another insect off the glass window with a **tap, tap** and flapped lazily away to the far bank. Well, that woke me up for sure! In the half-asleep dream-stage of early morning, my mind had filled in all the necessary details to turn my harmless visitor into a messenger of death. Now that was not the normal start to a day! I turned to see Yana staring at me.

"Are you alright Alex you look like you have seen a ghost?"
"For a moment I thought I had seen something just as bad."
"What?"
"A huge raven on the window."
"Alex you are such a twit, go and get dressed before you scare those fishermen."

I suddenly realised I was standing in front of the large glass window – naked! Certainly a worse shock for an Egyptian fisherman than a Nile raven.

After leaving Sid's home I was finished for the morning. I rushed back to my place and whipped off my socks. My feet had been freezing all morning! Yana just laughed at me being my usual *idiotic-self*. I spent the next half-hour sitting on the stairs with the hair drier set on maximum, wafting the heat over my toes and sipping warm sweet coffee. All I could wonder about was – how would the photo turn out?

Nile Ravens often dropped in to pick insects off the glass on our trip along the Nile.

STORM CLOUDS

"It will be another stormy day out at sea," Bella announced in a statement-like fashion as I was leaning over her Singer 514. She was gazing out towards the coast with a lost look on her face. "Wouldn't like to be a sailor today," she added under her breath, shaking her head slightly, "No not today."

I had the distinct impression that she would be talking even if I was not in the room. The way she was stroking her fat tabby-cat, snugly clasped under her arm like a set of Scottish bagpipes, it made me wonder if the conversation was even directed towards me.

I stood up and stretched my poor old aching back. Nearly a quarter of a century of bending over sewing machines had taken its toll on my spine and, at the slightest opportunity, it gave me payback. As I rubbed my stiff knotted muscles, I walked over to her with my cup of tea. It had been getting cold on her cluttered sideboard near the window. I looked out of the pretty cottage, through the leaded glass, out to the wild world that the walls of the cottage had kept at bay for three-and-a-half centuries.

"Yes it is a nasty day today for sure," I said as I came up to her. The cat lifted its head for a stroke. I stopped rubbing my back and tickled the cat under his chin, he purred away in satisfaction. I seemed to break her trance and we watched together, for a while, outside the bare branches of the high trees danced in a wild, rhythmical motion. Slaves to the whim of the wailing wind that raged.

Far in the distance, as the hillside dropped away, the sea looked cruel and furious. The wind had grown in strength for several days churning up the tempestuous deep, bringing in the big rollers that the fearless surfers love to ride. White horses raced over the dark ridges of the enormous waves, skipping from peek to peek in a stampede of untamed abandon. Huge waves, whose temper had grown in the far Atlantic, taunted by a cutting wind, rolled up the English Channel unopposed only to vent their rage upon the white cliffs that protect our fortress island. Like a glass thrown against a stone fireplace they exploded in sudden violence then fall away, all anger spent.

There was something very warm and comforting about being in the small cottage with the elements raging outside. We watched while the raindrops chased each other down the glass and the wild wind shook the garden plants. With my height I had to stoop a little to see clearly out of the small windows. Cottages like this one were built when the average height rarely exceeded five feet. Poor diet and unreliable seasons were not conducive to lots of growth. It is a modern phenomenon, indeed, that the average height of a human in areas of the world where food is now abundant has risen by as much as 12 inches.

"See that old tree over there?" she said pointing to a large bare tree dancing in the corner of a far field. "The walnut tree. My great grandfather planted it over a century ago. Many times, as a child, I climbed up her branches with my brothers and sisters to pick walnuts for pickling. It was my dad's favourite *after dinner* snack. He would sit in front of that old fireplace there," she said waving towards the cottage wall. "Kick off his shoes, slide on his old slippers, pour himself a tot of rum and open up a jar of mum's walnuts to nibble on. Then he would stare into the fire for hours, watching the *fire fairies* dance, never a word spoken – never a word."

"Happy memories," I added looking at the cold, dark, fireplace that just itched to be alight once again.
"Oh yes, happy memories indeed! I remember my old dad saying to me, come the time we had to break the branches of the walnut tree; *A woman, a dog and a walnut tree, the more they're beat the better they'll be.*" We both smiled at the old saying that would soon be forgotten in our modern world. The middle of winter is such a desolate time for so many of us. It is amazing to think that our ancestors lived outside, amongst the wild winds and howling beasts.

****

Long before Christianity came to our shores, old rituals would take place in the darkest time of the year. It was a simple task to place a few sticks into the ground and see where the sun rose each morning and to know when our giant star had decided to change its winter decent back towards the warmer summer months. Pagan man knew these times well and later religions such as the Druids, improved upon these methods, and erected stone monuments, which were carefully placed to measure the sun's movements throughout its yearly cycle.

Imagine a scene from midwinter that would have been performed around the shortest day of the year, when all seemed dead outside. When the world, as they knew it, had perished in the cold months of deep winter. Village folk would bring in some of the few living plants that were still left alive, like the deep green branches of the holly tree. They would clear away the animals from the centre of the floor and place the holly down upon the cold hard earth. A roaring fire would be blazing away as the head of the family started a ritual dance around the holly. As one of the family members beat on a dry skin, stretched over a twig frame, the rest would stamp the earth beneath their feet and dance around the holly. They stamped hard to awaken their sleeping mother, *mother earth*, and remind her to return to them. To once more, bring warmth for their crops to grow. Then, as the dancing reached a crescendo, the head of the family would throw the holly onto the fire. They would all pray as they watched it crackle and burn.

Of course this ritual always worked. For, shortly after the midwinter dance, the days would start to get longer and the sun would hold a promise of the warmth that it would soon bring to the frozen lands. To this day ancient boundaries in England are still marked by holly trees.

✳✳✳✳

I left Bella, with her tabby cat under her arm, still standing by the window. Entranced by the spectacle of nature at its wildest in the bleak midwinter. As I quietly pulled the door closed I wondered how long it would be before she realised that I had called to fix her machine?

THE FRIENDLY VILLAGE

January 13th 2002 was a good day. Foot & mouth disease was officially over at last. No more cases of diseased animals had been reported for weeks and the Ministry had given the countryside the *all clear*.

I was delighted. It had been such a hard time for all country folk. I had seen their never-ending struggle to survive and, even though we had no cases of the dreaded disease in East Sussex, the restrictions were as tough for us as anywhere else.

There is something so good about having Christmas behind you and the knowledge that each day, daylight will be staying a few minutes longer. There is a feeling that spring is on the way and the worst is over. Of course, we are usually wrong! But, at least, there is the thought that, when the weather does go from bad to worse, it will not be for long.

I was subconsciously looking for any signs of colour as I drove down the back road from Newick towards my next call at Barcombe. My previous call had been a perilous one. I had arrived a few minutes early and the husband ran downstairs to let me in.

"She won't be a moment Alex, you have just caught her in the shower. Go right in. You know where the machines are. Just get started on them and she'll be with you shortly. I'm off for another hour's kip in bed."

He then disappeared back up the stairs, his dressing gown flapping behind him. I walked into the living room and put my toolbox down. I could hear all the commotion upstairs as the family rushed around but it soon settled down. I had just started the first machine when I happened to glance across the living room. To my absolute horror there was a trail of muddy footprints. I looked down at my shoes and sure enough there was a blob of mud on the sole of my left shoe. I can tell you, the mud did not enhance their lovely cream, dining-room, carpet.

I went into my usual *panic-mode*. I slipped both shoes off and chucked them at the front door. Then I rushed to the kitchen sink. I grabbed the cloth from the sink and added a bit of *Fairy* washing-up liquid. The chubby little baby that was cheerfully smiling up at me from the bottle was in contrast to how I felt. My heart was pounding. I dropped to my knees and started on the first of nine splodges of mud that lead straight to my toolbox. I swear I could hear the theme tune to *Mission Impossible* pounding in my brain. I desperately rubbed away one after another. As I was frantically working, I could hear **my** customer moving around upstairs, which just made things worse for me. I had gone from *panic* to *super-panic* mode!

As I got to the last muddy footprint, I heard the dreaded sound of the stair's creaking. The lady of the house was coming down! I finished off, ran on tiptoes to the kitchen. No time to get to the sink! I launched the cloth towards the sink. It landed on one of the cyclamen pot-plants on the kitchen windowsill. The plant was minding its own business, happily flowering away, when the cloth landed straight on top of it. Nothing I could do about that now. I rushed back to the machines a second before Mrs Roberts entered the room. She had a white dressing gown on and was rubbing her hair with a towel as she walked in.

"Good morning Alex. You caught me out again. Every time you call you seem to be early. Next time I shall have to set my alarm clock half-an-hour before I need to."

I nodded back and smiled. I was gasping for breath – but trying not to show it – breathing in and out through the side of my mouth that she could not see.

"Would you like a drink Alex?" She continued.
"Love one." I muttered back through my clenched teeth.
"Alex, you look a bit flushed are you feeling all right?"
"Oh yes! It's just coming in from the cold outside, does that to me. I'll be fine in a second or two."
"Well, I shall get you a nice cup of coffee to settle you down."
Thankfully, she turned and walked off to the kitchen. I gasped a huge sigh of relief.

As she left, I looked down at the wet blotches on the carpet, mixed in with her wet footprints they were perfectly disguised. I could hear her muttering to herself in the kitchen.

"That useless husband of mine has been using the kitchen cloth to clean his boots and then thrown it over my favourite plant! I shall give him such a whack! He will think Christmas is back again."

Oops! I thought, still better him than me!

All I hoped was that I could get out of the house before he came down. Which I did – that will teach him to have an extra hour's sleep. The thought of her poor bewildered husband being blamed for the crushed houseplant brought a sneaky smile to my face as I drove away.

The village I was heading for was really Barcombe Cross and if you look it up on a map you will see it marked so. But we all know it as just Barcombe. Back in the *Middle Ages*, when famine and strife were commonplace, when plague and pestilence were a real and genuine fact of life, Barcombe succumbed to a terrible fate. *The plague* hit the main village, which is now no more than a farm and a few out buildings. The village, of around 150 people mostly of families 8 to 10 strong, was devastated. The beautiful and picturesque church of St Mary the Virgin is all that remains to show where a thriving village once stood. The villagers that suffered such a terrible fate lay in old, unmarked graves.

The Great Plague was an outbreak of *old bubonic plague* or *black death* from the 14th century. The plague only lasted a couple of years but wiped out about a quarter of the population in South East England.

People say that up until *The Plague,* when you died they used to bury you about two feet deep. But, after *The Plague*, such was the fear from contamination all bodies were buried six feet deep. A tradition that continues to this day. The mark of the plague was a red cross on your door. The bodies were taken away at night to the call of *"Bring out your dead."*

St Mary's has some lovely old features. Well, dating back to the 13th century, it would! Wouldn't it? There is a Spanish chest in the church with an amazing lock. Locals say that it floated up the river sometime after the defeat of *The Spanish Armada*.

Barcombe was a Saxon village that grew barley for that age-old nectar of all good fighting men – *ale*. Although recent archaeological digs have unearthed a Roman villa from the 1st century AD. It is in the heart of the rich and fertile flatlands that lay beneath the South Downs. The highly productive soil, watered from the River Ouse, was ideal for barley crops. When *The Plague* hit, the villagers that survived, burned the old village to the ground to remove all traces of the disease. They built a fresh village at the place it is today, Barcombe Cross. We can only imagine the pain that the small community went through centuries ago when half of all the village families went to an early grave. It is one of the great human achievements to overcome all obstacles and survive. We are all here today because our ancestors had that fighting spirit. The spirit never to give up however bad things became.

Barcombe at one time, had a Dr Barnardo's Home for Girls. Dr Thomas John Barnardo went to London from Dublin in the Victorian era. As a young and energetic doctor, he had intended to travel on missionary work to China but he was so appalled at the conditions he found London children living in, he stayed to help. He opened a home for orphaned children and gave them a chance for a better future. This was in a period of British history when the probability of a child reaching their fifth birthday stood at less than 50%.

In Barcombe, many of the girls married local men. One funny tale that survives from the war was when some Canadian service men were billeted near the village. Unfortunately, several of the young women fell pregnant. A furious commander marched the whole troop out in front of the girls and asked the up-and-coming mothers to point out the culprits. Guess what! They all pointed to the same man!

****

All was bleak as the Land Rover sloshed its way along the muddy roads towards the village. There was not even a dash of sunlight for the shiny holly leaves to catch and throw back in my direction. The other trees were bare and dormant, most of the wildlife was in hibernation or had fled to warmer climes. In the few fields that **did** hold cattle and sheep, they all looked thoroughly miserable as they clung, in small groups, to the far corners in search of some shelter. The crows sat in their bare treetop homes, like tenants with vacant possession, hunched over and bored from the endless drab days of winter.

In all the years that I had travelled around East Sussex, I had never found a village as friendly as Barcombe. Long forgotten was the terrible fate of the early villagers. Most locals probably do not even know why the village is split up like it is. It is still a small village, no more than a few hundred people. Not much bigger in size than when it was recorded in the Doomsday Book in the 11th century. Barcombe is just a stone's-throw from Lewes, our lovely county town but you could be forgiven if you believed that you had travelled back a century or more when you enter the village. As with all thriving villages, the village stores, church, school and pub are the focal-points of all village life. It is where locals meet and chat about such important tasks as who is going to judge the flower show this year and organize the Christmas carol service. Villages like these have the **four**, all-important, ingredients known in Sussex as the **four Ps**, Post Office, Pub, Parson and Parish School.

Barcombe Cross is no more than a pinprick on the map, blink twice and you will miss it. It is one of those places that you really have to search out and explore to fully enjoy. For example, down a very small lane hardly wide enough for a car, you will find The Anchor Pub. This picturesque, quintessentially English pub is set on the edge of a very pretty part of The River Ouse. At the pub, you can have a superb lunch outside by the river, then take a punt and wile away a summer afternoon drifting aimlessly along the river under boughs of sweet birch, willow and chestnut. Long ago Mr Brown – the landlord – would call to you as a punt became free and he would help you aboard. It was, and still is, the perfect way to spend a sunny afternoon.

As I arrived at my customer's house, Val was red-faced. She was busy with her *Benson's magic marmalade cutter.* A Victorian contraption for shredding the bitter peel of the Seville oranges. You put roughly cut chunks into one end and move the wooden handle back and forth. Out of the other end falls perfectly shredded rind.

"Can't get these contraptions for love nor money today!" Val said puffing away vigorously, attending to her machine with a sort of midwife efficiency.

She had a bright cotton apron tied around her large and happy midriff. On which, random splodges of orange juice, had made a sporadic pattern. There were even a few on her blouse. She seemed used to it, her sleeves rolled up to her elbows and a white cap covering her blonde-grey hair.

On the stove was a big preserving pan. The wonderful, bittersweet, aroma of fresh marmalade filled the room as the syrup bubbled away in the aluminium cauldron. Val stopped to lift some of the frothy scum away that had gathered around the edge of the pan with a big wooden spoon then went back to her puffing and panting on the shredder.

I got down to repairing her machine on the opposite end of the heavy, pine table. I pushed all the freshly-washed empty jam jars into the middle to allow just enough room for me to work. Over idle chatter I happened to mention about Barcombe being such a friendly village.

"Can't say it is any more friendly than any other village I know. In fact, it was not long ago that, if you were from one of the surrounding villages you would be called a *Frenchy* or *furrin*; basically a foreigner. All that has changed now, what with cars and planes and things. It's all very different today. When I was a nipper, you could spot a *Frenchy* a mile off. We used to keep a good eye on the Gypsies too. They would sometimes stray off the main road looking for work. We always knew what they were up to and where. Many a pheasant and hare fell to their traps as they passed by. Still all those times are long gone now. We even had an American couple looking for a place to stay in the village last year! Now that's progress for you!"

I had to laugh. American tourists, for heavens sake! Not long ago just the thought of such a person in a small village would bring children running across the fields – as they once did when they heard the roar of that new-fangled contraption that would never replace the horse, the motor car.

"Well it certainly seems to be a friendly village to me," I said licking my fingers with great satisfaction. I was enjoying a slab of crusty, buttered loaf, topped with lashings of marmalade that rested on top of the bread, as rich and appealing as a golden September sunset. In case of interrogation later, by Yana, I made a mental note to deny all knowledge of the snack, *I did not have relations with that crusty loaf!*

"Today one lady looked like her hand was going to fall off she was waving at me so hard. She was outside The Royal Oak, below the sign of Charles II. I am sure it was too early for her to be tipsy."

Val stopped her labelling of the jam jars and looked up at me for a moment. "Well, you do bear a passing resemblance to our village baker. That's probably who they are waving at. He drives a similar car to yours as well. Or rather he did. He has been desperately ill these last few months what with bypass surgery and blood poisoning. No wonder they are waving at you. They will be shocked at the sight. Mind you they'll be pleased that not only did you recover so well but back to driving... what with having a leg off an-all!"

So, that was it. All these years I had thought Barcombe was the friendliest village in Sussex and it was all down to me looking like someone they all knew? Well never mind, all in all it is a lovely village and at least, I do get a great reception there. I swigged down the last dregs of tea from my mug and polished off one more tempting morsel of bread.

I left Val with two pots of warm marmalade tucked under my arm. I could not help but wave at the old chap, on the corner of the road, who raised his cap and smiled so fondly at me. I am going to have to wear dark glasses and a cap if the baker dies, otherwise I will give half the village heart attacks. Looking better is one thing but back from the dead... well that's another kettle of fish!

Another typical country lane that I travel daily. There is no room for two cars, as you can see my Land Rover takes up all the road. Many times I have had to reverse to allow a car to pass. I wrecked the underneath of several cars on all the farm tracks that I use. That's why I bought the Land Rover.

A walk in the country in winter sunshine. This is the Jevington Stud with St. Andrew's Church in the distance, built over 1100 years ago. Notice the horses are all wearing horse rugs that have to be repaired regularly.

The Red Lion at Wish Hill, Willingdon. A great place for a pint and a bite to eat. Just down the road is the village pump house – the wall is made up of ox knuckles and no one knows why!

The Junction pub in Polegate, called The Junction as it lies opposite the Old Polegate railway station. This used to be a typical 'spit 'n' sawdust' pub and a good place for a pint of real ale.

The Castle is in Pevensey Bay. This pub has changed little since I was a child.

Sheila's Steakhouse, an old inn for travellers and one of the finest places for a good steak in Eastbourne. Just the sight of the inn makes me hungry!

One of my customer's horses with some local wildlife. Pheasants are reared yearly for shooting, but many escape and add a touch of colour to our countryside.

ERROL & IRIS
(A match made in heaven)

I had had a busy day planned and the calls were falling into some sort of order in my brain as I pulled into the early morning traffic. First call, Mrs Beecham, was just a quick one. A new bulb, and some needles, then off to Tye Barn Farm for a seized Singer. One more call to Mrs Whitton at the Warbill-In-Tun Inn then to Burwash. That would be about it for my morning.

Things got off to a bad start almost immediately when a police car came hammering down the wrong side of the road at an alarming speed, directly at me. The police car's occupants were clearly as alarmed as I was. The anti-lock brakes on the Land Rover bit hard into the juddering discs as I braked with all my might. The police car did the same and we came to halt within inches of each other. As I breathed a sigh of relief and blessed the dry road for my deliverance, the police car simply slipped into the traffic on its correct side of the road and roared away. Not a word of thanks. The driver in the car behind mine was more explicit. The woman, who had narrowly missed driving up my backside, gave the police car the good old British two-fingered salute as it shot away.

I carried on to my first call and then to my second. Iris Stevens was nowhere to be seen. I knocked on the front door then the back door – even the old shed in the garden – but no Iris! I looked across her farm towards the paddock where the horses had their heads stuck out of their stables, aimlessly watching the morning pass. Out towards the woods, which had started to bloom with wood anemone, throwing a white carpet over the woodland floor, I spotted Iris. She was staring into the woods, intently examining the thick undergrowth. I walked across the paddock over to her. As I approached I called "Mrs Stevens?"

She leapt into the air, dropping a heavy walking stick in the process. "My lord you put the fear of God into me Alex."
"Sorry, I could not find you anywhere. What on earth are you doing?"
"Would you believe looking for an escaped bull? It ran away last week and has been terrorising the walkers in the forest. We just cannot catch it. The beast has gone wild on us. It's that time of year you see, his blood is up and

he wants a few girlfriends. He must have got a whiff of the cows in the far pasture and just went wild on us. I am just so worried about him."

"Well that's a first, I must admit. How on earth do you think you are going to catch it?"

"No idea, simply no idea at all, 900 lbs of muscle and testosterone creeping around Lions Wood is enough to put anyone off their breakfast. I have seen plenty of his tracks but he has taken to hiding until nightfall, then roaming around like some ancient woodland beast. He has even made the horses nervous, not to mention the locals. We did get a rope around him a few days back but he dragged two of the lads a good 20 yards before they let go. He is a softie really – and so handsome. He reminds me of Errol Flynn the way his brown quiff of hair dangles over his strong, wide, forehead and those big soft eyes, ooh they can make you go weak at the knees."

I stood back and looked at Iris with my head cocked slightly to one side. Thoughts of early senility were rushing through my brain, Errol Flynn! For God's sake, it's a bull! What on earth is going on in there? I was just thinking she was one slice short of a loaf when she caught me staring at her out of the corner of her eye and quickly added, "No I have not eaten too much beef, I was just talking out loud, I am not completely mad…yet! We named him Errol when he was a calf for that very reason. I can have a soft spot for one of my animals can't I?"

"Perhaps there is an easy answer." I quickly spouted, trying to cover up my obviously transparent face.

"What do you mean?"

"Well, we all know the only thing that a young bull thinks about this time of year, besides food, is a few nice heifers. Put some cows in your best field of grass and he is bound to turn up for a *nibble*, so to speak."

Iris looked at me in a glazed astonishment as if I had just given her the winning lottery numbers for the week.

"Alex, you're a hero! I have been farming for 32 years and never thought of the most simple and obvious solution to my problem."

Simple…obvious? Hey! Less of the simple, I thought as I nodded, outwardly agreeing with her, if it was so simple why had she not thought of it, eh!

"I shall take a few lengths of fencing down by the woods over there," she pointed with a finger so crooked that I was only sure of the general direction. "I'll tie up a couple of my prime heifers. I feel positive that Errol will come-a-calling before long. Ah, I feel a great weight lifted off me. Well done! Now let's get the kettle on and make you a well-deserved cup of coffee," she said patting me on the back with several resounding smacks full of renewed vigour and energy.

Iris picked up her huge walking stick – that now made sense why she was carrying it, though I doubt a bull would feel much of a smack from her – and we marched happily back up the field across to her horses. "Wait one moment while I give Maisy her feed could you Alex?"
"Sure, no problem, she must be getting on a bit now isn't she?"
"Only 34," she laughed back, in a much more relaxed mood.

As we arrived at Maisy's stable, Iris bent over and picked up a small cream stone. "Oh Maisy you have gone and dropped another one you silly girl! What are you going to do if you lose all your teeth, eh, my pretty one?" She said rubbing Maisy's nose. Iris opened her hand to reveal a large, yellow tooth that had seen many better days. Then she reached down into her rough old waxed, green working coat, down into the huge pockets that were below her knees and pulled out a whole handful of teeth. "All Maisy's you know. Still, she has just enough left to see her through this season on hay. Next year we will start with the special feed that will not need so much chewing."

I looked at old Maisy whose big eyes almost glowed as Iris ran long loving strokes down her neck. I could not help wondering how many extra years Maisy had lived with the special love and care she had embracing her.

Back at the farmhouse I settled comfortably into servicing the Singer in front of the warm cooker that was throwing out its welcome heat. The kitchen smelt of fresh bread and the meaty stew that was bubbling away on the stove. I sipped coffee – with just the one sugar – as Iris excitedly phoned her friends to tell them of her plan to capture the bull. I could not fail to notice how it had become her brilliant plan. Each time she told another friend she kept repeating, "So simple when you think about it."

By the time I was ready to leave I had come to the conclusion it was better that it became her idea as everyone would be saying to her how simple it all was for the next six months. I was a little sad in a way as it would not have taken long before the wild bull's fame would spread across the land and the *Lions Wood Beast* would shoot into legend. You know what they always say? Legend is little more than gossip plus plenty of time thrown in.

As it turned out the silly young bull did not last out the day. Errol's quest for freedom was greatly outweighed by his urge to frolic with some tethered cows. I suppose the opportunity was just too good to miss. Supper and sex, all in one field. The beast was caught lustfully creeping into the top field just before nightfall on the very same day I visited. No, unfortunately, the Lions Wood Beast would not climb the immortal staircase into legend. So much for willpower against testosterone. At least the forest walkers will not have to run for their lives, chased by a brown-eyed, rampant bull with lust on his mind, quiff and all.

The Warbill-In-Tun pub at Warbleton looked warm and inviting as I climbed the steps past the *Egon Ronay* good-food plaque on the wall. Mrs Whitton's Husqvarna had locked into reverse while she was finishing off a christening gown and I was on a mission of some importance.

I love empty pubs in the morning. The cleaner had all the chairs upside down on top of the tables and some pushed up against the door. I tried to wiggle my way in. The Hoover was humming away, being swept back and forth in an easy motion by a trained hand. I nodded to her as I made my way up the small stairs beside the kitchens. Memories of one of my meals at the pub came flooding back. Crispy roast duck and plum sauce on a bed of superb vegetables made my mouth water. A good meal, with friends around a roaring fire in a country pub is just about as good as it gets for me.

With hunger pangs digging deep into my belly, I kept my mind on my job and went to work on the machine upstairs. Within the hour I was back in my trusty steed, whizzing along the back roads past several of Mad Jack's architectural follies that dot the landscape around the area, then by Rudyard Kipling's old home at Batemans and onto Burwash.

The area of land between Herstmonceux and Burwash is really the farming heartland of East Sussex. Some of the pages on my ordinance survey map for the area show dozens of farms, and few villages, set out over the rolling fertile land. It is a land of twisting country roads and endless sign posts planted on a thousand tiny junctions. The signposts, which are absolutely essential to all but the local inhabitants, remind me of white-gloved Italian traffic police. They stand proud on little mounds of turf at every junction and every turning, pointing the right way for the bemused traveller. During periods of war nearly all signposts were removed to slow up any invasion. They would have done much better just to turn them all around. The invaders would be going round in circles until they had got so fed up they would have gone home, or stopped off at the first pub they found and got drunk.

My last call of the morning in Burwash went swiftly and I turned my good old Land Rover back towards the coast and home for lunch.

"Your call after lunch has just cancelled," Yana told me as I walked in the door. "Her husband has gone in for a triple-bypass and he is the one who does the sewing. She said she would give you a ring in a few weeks if all goes well."

The thought of open-heart surgery made me shudder. *Good luck to the old boy*, I silently thought as I made my way towards the kettle.

Suddenly the busy day did not seem so daunting and an easy afternoon was on the cards. I had an hour or two to kill between sewing machine appointments. It is always funny how a single cancellation to a busy schedule can really throw a spanner in the works. I often find, that if I have spare time on my hands, that was not planned, I pace up and down like a restless father in a maternity ward. However, today, spring was in the air and I suddenly felt the urge to get up into the green hills of Sussex.

"Let's whip up onto the Downs for a walk and get some fresh air." I suggested to Yana. Rolly's ears stood to attention. All of a sudden the dozing mutt, that had seemed dead to the world only moments earlier, was hovering around my ankles eagerly panting. I looked down at the pleading eyes and fiercely wagging tail, my mind was made up. We grabbed our coats, the dog lead and hit the road.

The wind had been blowing from the southwest, bringing the fresh salty smell of the sea with it. As it swept over the downland, it lifted the sound of the church bells from the town below. Spring was really bursting. Winter had passed quickly and easily this year. Last summer on the downland was still a hazy memory, the way the chalk-grassland flowers swayed to an invisible tune as the warm summer breeze tickled their stems. How sweet the purple orchids and rampions looked as they danced together among the green carpet of rough grass, while cowslips dipped and bobbed in rhythm with the contented sighing of the gentle wind.

As we walked I saw my first skylark of the year, it hung above me in the cool thermals, singing it's little heart out with a tune so sweet that it could make a grown man cry. I gazed over the fertile hills, down the steep escarpments that drop away with thick woodland to the sides of the hills and smiled, What a view I thought breathing in deeply. As we strolled, I recounted my morning's tale to Yana, of Iris and Errol – her wild handsome bull with his big brown eyes and hair all in a quiff.

Rolly was busy chasing shadows in front of us, cast down from the bright cotton-wool clouds onto the fresh turf below. I laughed out loud as we walked across the high open hills of Sussex. Thoughts of scatty old Iris kept springing to mind, romping through the woods, hand-in-hand or rather hand-in-hoof together with Errol, her true love, with a chewed wood anemone hanging seductively from the side of his sly, wide, mouth.

In the downland shrub the gorse was in full bloom. Its bright yellow flowers bursting with vibrant colour just like the joyous daffodils in the valleys. Japonica was flowering in the bushes, as was the wild cherry. The first tiny orchids had popped their heads up to have a look around.

We walked with light feet on the soft, fresh, grass. There was a smell in the air, a fresh wholesome smell. It was the smell of the downland growing, of a thousand million blades of grass, each bursting with fresh growth for a new year. Each individual blade was letting out the tiniest aroma that was almost impossible to notice. But put the scent of each one together and multiply it a million million times, then throw it onto the cool spring breeze that was rushing over the undulating green hills from the wild sea. That is when you have something special. You have the smell of heaven. Yes! Spring was really here in East Sussex and things were looking good.

A wonderful Bee Orchid. Finding this on the downland was a pure delight.

A Common Orchid, another regular to our roadside verges. This year a councillor strimmed a whole bank down thinking they were weeds. Needless to say he was a touch embarrassed when the Village in Bloom judges came to inspect the orchids.

The Rushlake Green signpost – a typical signpost. We would all be lost without these little gems in our countryside.

AL's Alfriston Travel Guide

I wonder if you have ever thought about the word – *breathtaking*? It is one of the words that I occasionally use to describe a place. I do not use the word lightly, it is one of the words that I hold in highest esteem. I use it when I am describing somewhere that really does take your breath away. A place where you stop, stand and stare. A place where, for a few seconds, you really do stop breathing.

I am blessed that the area where I was born has several of these places. Places that are simply magical in their quality. We all know places that are like that, some are world famous like the *Grand Canyon, Victoria Falls* or the *Pyramids* at Giza. Some can be just around the corner from your home and are magical to you. There are also times of day, sights and sounds that are magical. Sunrise and sunset, a full moon over the ocean, dawn over a desert, the *Northern Lights*, a shooting star, a warm wind through a field of ripe grain, rain after a hot dry spell and a thousand more, all priceless.

After I finished book two in the *Random Threads* trilogy *Skylark Country*, a publisher Nicholas Battle from *Countryside Books*, asked me if I would like to write a travel guide for him about East Sussex. I thought about it for a long time while writing this book and then an idea came to me. I thought, why don't I write about one of my favourite journeys around my area and see how it goes. I may well write the travel guide. After all, it is not often that a publisher of such esteem comes knocking on your door and asks you to write a book!

So, after much consideration, I decided to describe a journey from my local giant, the *Long Man of Wilmington* that I have mentioned many times, to just beyond the village of Alfriston. A short journey of some 4 miles or so that takes in some of the most breathtaking scenery in East Sussex and a lot of history to boot. This piece will be quite long but broken up into sections and mainly descriptive. You know what they say, *the Devil is in the details*. I hope you enjoy it. Anyway, I won't give up my day job just yet!

Wilmington

To start off we are going to walk from *The Giant's Rest*, a great country pub just off the A27 Lewes to Eastbourne road, to the pretty Sussex church of *St Mary & St Peter*. It is a wonderful walk on a quiet day, through the village of Wilmington, a village that has changed little in centuries. Wilmington gets its name from a Saxon that settled and farmed the land called Wilma – now that name sounds familiar – *Wilma I'm home*! Hey, how did Hollywood get hold of the name?

The narrow village road is one of the most picturesque in my part of Sussex. Although all the old traders of earlier years have long gone, the cottage names sometimes point to the trades that were carried out there. Bakers, blacksmiths, butchers and candlestick makers. The road still has its drainage ditch, running along side the houses, where you would slop out your undesirable waste each day. It is a real joy to walk along the shaded street looking at all the lovely country houses and cottages.

Many ghost stories abound in this area and it would not be too hard to imagine some ghostly figure floating along this old lane late at night. One ghost was said to be that of an old, one-legged, sailor who was supposed to haunt the road. Many times his wooden leg has been heard clonking along the cobbled street after dark but, when people would go to look no one was there. Then there is, of course, the traditional old lady who is supposed to glide along through the gardens following spectre-like images into the night. All these old stories were probably made up by mothers to make sure their children were in before dark and home in time for supper.

Mind you, I say that but one of my customers, who lives in the shadow of the old Priory, has had several unexplained encounters with the ghost of a young girl. In fact, one day the ghost became so annoying, what with all the locking of doors and the turning of pages in her books that she shouted at the ghost to grow up and stop fooling around. It must have upset the young girl for she has not been to visit since.

St Mary and St Peter

The beautiful flint church of *St Mary and St Peter* was built around the 12th century right next to a Benedictine priory known as *Wilmington*

Priory. The priory was one of the casualties of Henry V's wrath. Although the priory survived from the 13th to the 15th century, it finally fell into ruin. Many priories suffered at the hands of our kings, especially Henry VIII. This was because they held tremendous lands and thus power over the common people. In the olden days, land was not just wealth but power. All wealth came from the land. For the Stock Market and white-collar workers in the huge cities of today it would have been the stuff of dreams. He who controlled the land controlled the country. So Henry decided to gain control by the simple task of flattening all opposition. A ruthless but successful tactic. Hence, our poor Benedictine monks fled back to Normandy and the priory was destroyed. The few buildings and flint walls that remain are testament to those turbulent political times and to the quality of building techniques. The dilapidated walls that once resounded to the rejoicing of monks, now provide shelter for pigeons.

The pretty little church is such a sight to behold. Nestling in a small coppice of woodland almost unseen from the road. There will be many books that tell you all about what was built, when and by whom. What I want you to see is the charm and peace of the place. Inside there is a feeling of quiet rest, of harmony and great age. It is easy to imagine how many couples walked up the aisle, starting their married life together. The bride would be wearing a garland of flowers picked from the hedgerows and fields outside. The bridegroom, with a glowing smile, would wrap his arm in hers and walk the short walk to the doorway while all the villagers, young and old, cheered and clapped. The happy couple would be showered with flower petals as they made their way to the local pub for food, drink and dancing late into the night.

If you ever visit the church, take a second to stop and think about the people who lived here. How many times would the local community have come together in times of joy and grief? Think about all the priests that would have knelt before the altar to give praise for a good harvest or a long life. Wonder how many times the church bell would have been tolled to summon everyone to prayer? The church was the centre of village life. As I have said many times, communities would revolve around the main focal points of village life like the church and the pub.

In Wilmington you are walking through history. Stepping in the footsteps of old Sussex folk and seeing what they would have seen. They are but shadows and dust now but their toil, their work in the fields and along the hedgerows, their presence in the buildings and landscape is still here for all to enjoy. Take a moment to stand in silence. Walk outside amongst the gravestones and read out the names of villagers, like Ade who probably would have travelled, in their entire lives, no more distance than to the markets at Hailsham or Lewes. Those villagers knew little of the outside world but everything about the area in which they lived and died. They were in tune with the seasons and ran their lives by the daily rising and setting of the sun. Amongst all of this, in the centre of Wilmington village life, was this little church.

In the church graveyard is a magnificent yew tree. It has stood there since before King Harold was slain at Hastings in 1066. It stands with outstretched limbs sagging. Limbs that have known more than a thousand years of recorded history come and go. I wonder what sights it has seen and what graves have been dug beneath those aching limbs. It keeps its secrets. Did it not cry out as the gravedigger's spade caught those strong roots as he cut into the fertile soil to lay another local to rest? Old and tired it stands proud, guarding the souls of the departed. It is part of our pagan heritage that has been allowed to continue into Christian times and legend has it the limbs help guide the spirits of the departed to the afterlife.

Out the back of the churchyard is a magnificent view of the Sussex Weald. The view is a slice of heaven. If you take a deep breath you can smell the Sussex air and taste the rich soil. I once bumped into an old man that had come all the way from Canada to see the place where his dear departed wife had spent her childhood. He was sitting on a stone bench just behind the graveyard all on his own. Typically, I was sneaking around the back of the church with a meat pastie that I had bought from Polegate and was looking for somewhere tranquil to enjoy it.

He told me that he had to come and see the place that his wife had described with such love and passion. They had always planned to return together but fate had intervened. He was so happy to meet me as I could tell him where all the places were that she had mentioned. We ended up sitting for an hour on the hard seat sharing my pastie and reminiscing on life. Meetings like those with complete strangers who, just for a brief second, share their life with you are so fascinating.

The Long Man of Wilmington

Right now, I am going to take you up the small hill past the remains of the old Priory to what is now a car park. This is where we get the best view of our white giant clothed in green. I will tell you all about him. Don't be scared he does not bite! He always looks his best with the afternoon sun on him. What is his name I hear you ask? He is now called *The Long Man of Wilmington*. What his real name was has been lost through the folds of time.

What we know of our local giant is scanty to say the least. There are a hundred different theories that have come up over the years. The first documentation of him comes from an illustration from the early 18th century. So we must ask ourselves is he older than that? Because of the regular maintenance of his outline over the years it is impossible to date him using traditional carbon dating. Also, in the summer of 1870 the *Archaeological Trust* decided to enhance his outline with white painted bricks. Before this period his form would go unseen for long periods of time. Locals would be working in the fields and when the light was just right, they would look up to see the giant appear then disappear just as quickly. It must have given the magnificent *old man of the hills* a real magical touch. We must wonder at whom or why people would make such a giant. The facts are simple. He is almost 230 feet (60 m) tall and carved out of the chalk hillside with a significant degree of skill. This only becomes apparent from standing close at the base of our giant. The proportions are so cleverly devised that, from a distance, he is a very good outline of a human and you do not realise how huge he is until you are right next to him. Standing at his feet looking up you can see that he has been elongated on the sloping hillside. He is one of the largest representations of the human figure in the world. Not bad, eh?

Is he an ancient god or a giant that lived long ago? Is he holding staves, divining rods, or battle staffs? Could he even be holding open the gates to another world? Could he be striding across the swollen River Cuckmere, with his staves for support, to rescue villagers from a great flood? The Cuckmere valley has a tidal river, at its centre, that is prone to flooding. Was he carved to pacify old demons, an ancient deity or was he carved to celebrate a grand victory or just as a local hero or simply to ensure a good harvest? There are certainly many more questions of him than answers available. But if you are ever there as the sun drops, and Windover Hill becomes dark against the night sky, there is a magic in the air, a power, that you can feel through your very bones.

He is set into an unnaturally flat-topped hillside that has been flattened. Was it an old flint site of Neolithic man or a chalk pit used by the Romans for one of their favourite building ingredient, concrete? Could the hillside have been left like a blank landscape just itching for an enthusiastic artist to create a giant? Could a few of the monks from the abbey be filling in some spare time by carving out a giant? The list is endless. You could get a wonderful selection of quite plausible answers by going to a pre-school classroom and asking all the children where he came from.

There is one, rather rude, point worth mentioning that throws into dispute his 18th century roots. If you happen to see The Long Man early in the morning after a sharp frost a rather impressive appendage appears, showing that his original form was far more revealing than his present one. Over the years he has often been defaced or rather repainted by *visitors in the night* that have added his grand assets back. Are they subconsciously putting him back to how he really did look?

If he was originally a well-endowed fellow then he certainly would not have been carved in the prim and proper Georgian-Victorian era when showing an ankle was deemed inappropriate. Also, to back this theory up, when the Australian and New Zealand troops were stationed at nearby Peacehaven. Peacehaven was formerly known as *New ANZACS* – because of the Australian and New Zealand troops. Many of the soldiers who helped clear local scrub and downland went back and told their families of the giant that, when properly cleared, included his full manhood. And why would old descriptions of him say *He stands naked before the shires?* Even Kipling used this phrase. Was the Long Man, the first ever sex change?

White witches – the friendly sort that have strong roots with *mother earth* – have held ceremonies at the foot of the *Giant*, as have the Druids. There are plenty that believe he has healing powers and many have claimed our Long Man as their own. In my mind I have no doubt that he is of ancient origin but proving if he is 500 or 5000 years old is a difficult task. This is my personal belief after seeing him, all of my life, lying quietly in the soft green of the downland and serenely gazing over the farmlands below. He watches us, as we rush through our hectic lives, as no more than ants below his feet.

All around this area it is rich in pagan history. In Berwick churchyard, hardly a stone's throw away, stands a pre-Christian worship stone. Neolithic man was known to have flint mines near this spot and their burial grounds are dotted over the high places of the Downs. I do believe that ancient man gazed upon our giant, as we do today.

Although his origin has been lost to us over the centuries and his secret history hidden for now, there is no doubt that our colossus stands proud as the protector of these superb ancient lands.

Lullington and Litlington

From Wilmington we are going to travel along the narrow road towards the hamlet of Lullington, which then leads on to Litlington. The name comes from a Saxon farmer who settled here. He was apparently a tiny fellow known, not surprisingly, as *Little*. He had a *tun* or *farmstead*, so hence the name *tun*. When English was standardized by the printers it became *ton* and so, as a quick guide to the area, if you see a sign finishing in *ton*, like Alfriston, then it is safe to assume that many years ago Alf – originally Aelfric – had his farm there.

In fact most of our country was named after the people who lived in the area or a feature of the countryside that was easy to identify, like a bridge, a wood, a rise in the land, a marsh, or a pool. Easy when you think about it. If you were trying to tell a traveller where to go you would describe the places he had to pass. It could be a farmstead or a hollow, eventually the place would gain the name that would be common to all folk.

When William the Conqueror decided to tax the people properly, he commissioned the first *official* survey of the country. Scribes and officials were sent to every corner of the land to find out who owned what, what monies were earned in rent, who fished which ponds for eel and pike and a thousand other details. The names that were locally referred to were, from then on, documented in the *Doomsday Book*. Hence, simple names like *Wilma's farm* became part of the written word and ended up, a thousand years later, as Wilmington.

I guess you get the picture so I won't rattle on too much about it. I am always wondering where the names of towns and villages come from and, even more so, the names of people. So many names were just from their trades. Sawyer would have been a woodsman. Cooper a barrel maker and so on. Arrowsmith, Blacksmith, Butcher and Baker, all referring to their trades. Fletcher was originally the man who attached the feathers to arrows, so Mr Fletcher always lived near Mr Arrowsmith. True! How many people do you know whose name tells of their old family's trades? There are plenty around when you start to look. I suppose our most famous was former Prime Minister, Maggie Thatcher, no prizes for guessing what her ancestors did for a living.

Once beyond the Priory and Long Man, farmland rolls before the road for miles. The fabulous South Downs fold out for a hundred miles towards the West Country and the Dorset coast. I always look upon the South Downs as the heart of Sussex. You can feel her pulse as she beats in time with the seasons. You can almost see her moods as she changes with the weather. Sometimes dark and brooding, sometimes light and carefree, always beautiful. On clear days you can have almost magical views of the downs and farmlands, which are so pretty that they have been called God's heavenly acre. In high summer, with the swifts gliding over the farmland and the corn swaying in the fields, it really is a breathtaking view.

Lullington Church

On a little further, we come to Lullington Church, built around 1220, once known as the smallest church in England. Guess what? A farmer called Lulla worked the land here over a thousand years ago. At one time the church – known as *The Church of the Good Shepherd* – was much larger. Fire destroyed the main building leaving only the entrance standing. The vicar, not wanting to lose his parish, converted the remains into the church we see today. With 20 seats and standing room, the church is nestled into the downland up a small path, a *twitten*. It is a lovely little church and easy to miss driving down the narrow lane but well worth a visit.

Right, let us get off to Alfriston. We are going to skip along past Plonk Barn and over Long Bridge where, on lazy summer afternoons, I would watch the mullet glide up and down the murky river and the swans drifting along, doing little more than looking elegant. In July of each year the Queen has a special task force that counts the Royal birds on the Thames. It is called the *Swan Upping*. The swan is a protected bird that, officially, only the Royals and their dignitaries are allowed to eat, hence they need to be counted. It is called *Swan Upping* as they invariably chase the swans up river to count them.

It is a lovely walk along the riverbank from Plonk Barn to Alfriston because much of the village's charm and the superb village church can be seen from the river walk.

Drusillas

Before we get to Alfriston I must mention the excellent wine centre, and Drusillas Zoo, just along the road a smidgen. If you are interested in wine then this is the place to visit as it has many fine examples from some of the 400 British vineyards that produce fine wines.

Drusillas is the most perfect place for children of all ages, from 4 to 104! You can spend the day, seeing all the animals and attractions they have to offer. Winner of the best *small zoo*, Drusillas really does put on a great show.

Alfriston – Part One

I am going to go into quite a bit of detail with Alfriston as it has a fantastic amount of history. The village nestles into the Cuckmere valley with ample grazing and the river close by. It really is the most ideal place for a village. If one were not there it would be created. Parking is not too good in the village so if you are visiting, park in the main car parks that you come to, on the outskirts of the village, at the bottom of North Street. Then walk into the village from there. It is only a short walk up to the High Street and there is lots to see on the way. In the car park you will notice the strange, conical, flint building. There are many ideas as to what it was used for, everything from a lock-up for the village drunks, to a furnace to produce lead shot in the Napoleonic wars. To me it looks like the many conical-shaped smoking sheds that are found up and down the country. Smoked eel was a delicacy that few would deny and the river is still an excellent source for eels.

If you ever get to Alfriston, on your way to the centre of the village note all the enchanting names of the houses and cottages. *Cinder Cottage, Pump Cottage, Chestnut Cottage, Twitten House, Lavender Cottage, Flint Cottage* and many more. They fit this pretty village perfectly. Alfriston is so full of delights that it would bring a smile to Ebenezer Scrooge. If you are in Alfriston when the first rays of sun rush up the Cuckmere valley and lift the drab-grey colours of the night with its orange glow, you could be forgiven for thinking that you had been transported back in time, to a place the world had forgotten.

The great chestnut tree that shelters the Market Cross beneath its boughs in the High Street is not quite so *great* now as they keep hacking it back to allow traffic through. In the winter it looks like a large, hairy, hand with its fingers chopped off. The tree was planted to mark the ascension of Queen Victoria to the throne in 1837. Though some doubt that this is the original tree, only a chainsaw could prove the argument conclusively!

The tree is a good place from which to describe Alfriston. It is a delightful, picturesque, village. One of the finest in the land and from the vantage-point of the market square you can see some of the village assets. I just love the charming little Post Office with its bright red facade. It just begs you to pop inside and buy some goodies, like a child with pocket money.

Alfriston, once again, gets its name from the first well-known inhabitant, a soldier who settled and worked the land called Aelfric. Apparently he was granted the land for services to his king, *Alfred the Great*, and his lands were certainly mentioned in the Doomsday Book. There is a legend that King Alfred (of burnt-cake fame) who had his stronghold down the coast in Winchester was actually hiding out in Alfriston when he made his famous error of falling asleep instead of looking after the cakes he was supposed to be minding. From then on, whatever the great king did, he would be remembered for burning the cakes and being chased off by a very unhappy maid.

King Alfred, famous for chasing those nasty spiked-helmeted Vikings out of Southern England to places like Normandy – Norse lands – was said to have had a palace around these parts. He may well have done. In those days a fire behind a stone-wall, with a bed of straw raised off the floor, could have been called a palace. In the period between Roman and Norman rule known as the Dark Ages there were few buildings of note. To my mind it was not until the French invasion with William that our architecture really exploded in grand style.

To enjoy Alfriston to the full you need to stroll around the village. There is an excellent selection of stopping places, from small coffee shops to inns. Many of the former offering a wonderful afternoon cream tea of jam scones and cream. Oh, I should not mention food, it makes me so peckish! Luckily, I have not managed to type and eat at the same time – yet. *The Wingrove Inn, Deans Place, Moonrakers, The Star Inn* – one of the oldest inn's in England – *The George Inn, White Lodge, Badger's Tea Rooms* and many more. Check out the bright-red ship figurehead on the corner of the Star Inn. It apparently came from a shipwrecked Dutch ship lured onto the rocks by false signal fires, then ransacked by infamous bands of smugglers…. Well, that's the locals' story.

The Smugglers and Market Cross

The Market Cross is next to the chestnut tree, opposite The Smugglers' Inn where they make a steak sandwich to die for. But make sure if you visit and have been tramping along the South Downs Way that runs straight through the village, that you take your muddy boots off. Many a traveller has had a funny look and a tongue-lashing for tramping mud into the pub.

The pub was once a haven for gangs of smugglers that slipped up the river in the dead of night with illegal produce from France, Spain and the Caribbean. If you get the tide just right on the Cuckmere, you can float up-river with the surge of incoming floodwater with little effort. The inn was not always called 'The Smugglers'. It would have been a bit of a giveaway really – especially to the excise men looking for the guilty parties involved in their illicit, nightly trade. It used to be called, appropriately, The Market Cross Inn.

The Smugglers' Inn has a profusion of doors, at least 47, that all lead to visions of smugglers running off, leaving half-finished pints of ale, their goods tucked under their arms as excise men came-a-knocking

I should say a little about the small unobtrusive Market Cross that coach drivers and lorry drivers curse. It is a very rare cross, indeed, with only a few left in the whole country. Built over 500 years ago, it was originally a much larger monument with a speaking platform from where the village crier would announce up and coming events, news and the twice-yearly village fairs. The Market Cross is in Waterloo Square that gets its name from the soldiers billeted around the village during the Napoleonic Wars. One point to note is that most mobile phones do not work in the village, because Alfriston is in a dip and signals are poor at best. If you need to phone someone, do it before you get into the village or use the pay phone.

See now. How many other travel guides would be so helpful? I think I am getting the hang of this now.

Each shop and dwelling in the old part of Alfriston has a story to tell. You could spend days examining every house and visiting every shop. They are all special. Opposite the Market Cross is an old-world gift shop that has a small history of Alfriston, as does the Clergy House that I shall get to in a jiffy.

St Andrews

You must take a visit to the gorgeous St Andrews Church, sitting upon a slight rise at the back of the village in front of the green known locally as The Tye. St Andrews, built around 1360, is just one of those simply perfect examples of an English church. Once again stories tell us that, when the building was first started, the stones were mysteriously moved each night to the present site of the church. Eventually the builders put it down to **godly** interference and built the church where it is today. Others say that four oxen were grazing on the Tye and when they sat down in the summer heat, to rest, they sat with their backsides facing each other in a perfect cross. Surely an omen!

That is supposedly why the church is built in the pattern of a Greek cross today. One other story is that St Anthony ordered the church of St Andrews to be built here after he had travelled up the river – which was much larger centuries ago. It even had barges with goods until 1915, hard to imagine today. St Anthony set foot on the soil at Alfriston and decided that there could be no finer place for a church, to be closer to God, than here in his beautiful garden.

St Andrews has been described, by many that have gazed over her ancient stones, as the *Cathedral of the Downs*. It is easy to see why. The church enjoys one of the finest positions for a church in all of southern England. The church was completed all in one go, which is unusual, as most churches have had many additions over the centuries. The centre of the church houses the bells. This means that ropes fall into the middle of the church, impractical to say the least, as the ropes are smack in the middle where the seating ought to be. That is probably why you do not see churches of this design very often. Pleasing on the eye, but impractical for daily use. Mind you, saying that, no one would ever change St Andrews for it really is a gem, a little cathedral.

In spring snowdrops grow in profusion over the banks of the graveyard where many a soul has come to rest. I could not imagine a more pleasant spot in which to lay my bones than at this church. Talking of bones, they say that long ago, around the end of the 7th century, a young girl called Lewinna died for her beliefs. Apparently she was hacked to death by ferocious Saxons who were often up to no good. She was laid to rest at the old church over which St Andrews was later built. When she was canonized, her remains were a popular visitors' attraction, much like Becket's in Canterbury. Many pilgrims believed her martyred body had sacred healing powers. Unfortunately, centuries later, her bones were stolen by a Belgian monk and taken abroad. So that was the end of the tourist trade in Alfriston for a thousand years or so. In the chancel are two carvings, one of a woman's face, it is said to be that of Lewinna herself.

If you ever get the chance, take a peek at the square-napped flint from which the church has been built. It is an old and skilled craft. Check out the excellent saints in the stained glass windows, and for the architects amongst you, check the 14th century King Post and chestnut beams. The north transept windows also have their original stonework. After you have admired the inside and all its charms, take a walk around the back of the church and sit awhile. Let the tranquillity of the area soothe your troubles away as you gaze across the green downlands of Sussex.

Alfriston Tye

Standing at the entrance to the church you get a marvellous view back over *the Tye* towards the village. The rooflines of all the properties are snuggled together and provide an architectural feast for those of you that love old buildings. They look like a scene from an old Victorian novel. There is an old, explosive, sea mine on the Tye that floated up the river one high tide. As you can imagine it caused quite a fuss and the village had to be evacuated until the mine was disarmed. Now it is just another harmless reminder of troubles past. The summer fayre held on the Tye is a sight to behold. The old games all come out, like *shove-ha'penny* and *tossing the hay bale*, even *tug o'war* returns, with feisty villagers pulling their heart out amidst cheering crowds.

Tables of homemade cakes and jams are on sale, plus many more things. All the money raised usually goes to needy local causes. The whole Tye, that can seem empty for so many months of the year, heaves with enthusiastic humanity as the fayre takes over village life for a whole week.

The Clergy House

Just next door to St Andrews is the 14th century Clergy House. The very first property ever purchased by the National Trust. In 1896 it cost the extortionate sum of £10. You don't get bargains like that any more. To be fair, it was in appalling condition at the time. This wattle and daub, thatched, timber-framed building (don't ask what daub is near supper time, it contains some smelly ingredients) is now the jewel in Alfriston's plentiful crown and an excellent example of early Weald building techniques. The floor was reproduced using an age-old method of crushing chalk and combining it with sour milk as a binding agent. I would not liked to have smelt that for a few weeks after completion. Still, it worked like a charm in many buildings.

Alfriston Revisited

Alfriston also had a thriving racing set. Even, once, having its own horse-hero when *Longset* won the Lincoln National. One of the village's flamboyant visitors was the Victorian entrepreneur, Horatio Bottomley. Although Horatio was raised in a modest family he set about burning a bright flame in his hectic and sometimes fraudulent career. He was considered to be the founder of tabloid journalism after buying the *Sun* newspaper in 1898 and founding the publication *John Bull* in 1906. Once tipped to be prime minister he had a lovely mansion at Upper Dicker, that is now part of St Bedes School.

Horatio's star burned bright but was fuelled with illegal dealings. During his prime he had several of his horses around Alfriston, though never managed to win any prominent races. Eventually his paper world – sorry a bit of a poor pun here – crumpled around him. He was declared bankrupt no less than four times during his colourful and turbulent career. The former Member of Parliament, once dubbed the *Napoleon of Finance*, lost everything and, in his failing years, was even refused an army pension. It was a sad end to a charismatic and popular local character.

Ghostly Goings On

Just before we leave Alfriston the village that has been described as all things to all people, I must tell you more about its ghosts of which there are several.

Of course, an ancient and colourful village, such as this, would have its fair share of ghouls. Most of the ghost stories are attributed to grisly deaths that have happened over the centuries. These, unfortunate victims, are not based so much on historical accuracies, but on word-of-mouth passed down over a pint of the frothy stuff around the fireside on cold winters' evenings in the local taverns. But, having said that, they all make a good story and you know what they say? There's no smoke without fire!

Many moons ago, one dark and windy night, a wealthy local boy and his dog made their way home along *White Way*. Suddenly he was set upon by a band of robbers. During his brave resistance he was cudgelled to death. The cut-throats hastily buried him near the roadside but, as they started to leave, they heard his faithful dog sitting beside the hidden grave, howling for his master. They returned and killed the dog. Then the haunting started.

When eve'n closes upon the day
And nightly shadows blend with grey
Then ghostly vapours haunt White Way

Every seven years the hound would appear and howl on the spot where his master met his death. If the dog was approached it would melt into the earth. On the deathbed confession of an old vagrant the bones of the young man were dug up and given proper burial at the church. However the sightings continue.

What about old Mildred Reed? She was heard calling for help. Nothing unusual there, except that she had been buried three days earlier. Her grave was hastily opened, only to find her departed corpse well and truly dead. But that did not stop the sounds continuing.

In many graveyards, in Victorian times, you could find graves that had a small bell above the headstone. The bell was attached via a string to the inside of the coffin. Just in case the inhabitant decided they wanted to get up. Now that would give a grown man a fright if one of those bells started ringing!

Then there was the old groom who worked the stables near the forge. He made spectral appearances around the stable block on several occasions, looking for his horses.

What about the kind old dear that tucks up visitors in their beds, only to disappear through the wall. How about that for extra service? And the elegant silk-dressed lady that often pops into Dean's Place. Dean's Place was once part of the 12th century Wilmington Priory, so it has early roots in the area. Around the turn of the last century the bones of a woman were discovered there. Could they have been the remains of our ghostly guest?

My favourite ghost of Alfriston is one that few but local people know about, an old shepherd and his dog. He is a friendly old chap that is quite visible as he walks with his faithful mutt up the old chalk road off Winston Street by *the old sanctuary.* You may never know that he is a ghost for he will stop and talk to you as his dog sits silently by his side. However, no sooner do you turn your back on him he disappears. His only give away is his old shepherd's apparel, smock and trilby hat not worn by shepherds for generations.

And last, but by no means least, The Smugglers' Inn has had its spectral visitors. Some are attributed to the infamous smuggler and former owner of the Inn, Stanton Collins – a devious smuggler. It is said that Stanton may even have led an excise man to his death over the cliffs on the coast. Several of his Alfriston gang met untimely deaths and some were deported to Australia. Was the figurehead on the corner of The Star Inn one of his predecessor's terrible deeds? Is the long-gowned lady, that has appeared, one of his acquaintances from long past?

We shall never know. But what we do know is that Alfriston has as many ghosts as an apple tree has apples in autumn and some just as colourful. I remember one of my customers telling me that a big burly builder came rushing in as white as a sheet, out of the back of the Smugglers where he was working. He downed two double whiskys before telling everyone how he had just said good afternoon to a woman who promptly disappeared through the wall.

One way to tell that she was a ghost is that her feet are never visible, it is as if she was walking along a different level to the one that exists today.

High and Over

Well, that's it for Alfriston. Now I am going to take you to a spot that will simply take your breath away. We are on our way from Alfriston towards Seaford on the coast. We are going to stop at a place known as The *High and Over*.

One of the best ways to really see the superb downland and stunning countryside is on foot. From the car park at the highest point above Seaford, there is a short walk through a small *spinney* to the beauty spot at Frog Firle known as Hindover Hill. We call that place the *High and Over* as you go up, *Hi-nd-over*, down the other side.

The best time to visit this majestic place is in the late afternoon. As the sun starts to cool and melt into the distant horizon behind you it lights up the Vale of Cuckmere. It surely is one of the most inspiring and beautiful places God put on this earth. Because we drive up some 400 feet (330 m) to the viewpoint, we stand like Olympians surveying the lands below. Cattle grazing in the Vale look no more than small, toy-size shapes and the swans in the river are specks of white.

Miles of open land, hills, forests and sea open out before your eyes in a heavenly blend of nature at its best. The scene is dominated by the Cuckmere river – which meanders through the landscape below, wriggling its way out to sea some four miles away at Cuckmere Haven.

In early morning, the light from a low sun throws a trillion diamonds into the sky off the sea. And in the late afternoon the same sun bathes the whole panorama in a soft golden glow. I have probably visited Hindover Hill a hundred times and each time I am awe struck. In winter the winds can come up the valley so cold and fast that they can cut you in half. Some days the whole view is lost in mist. I have been there on a morning when a thick fog obscured everything below – but above me was a clear blue sky. After heavy rain is always the best time for a good view as the rain cleans the air, removing all the tiny dust particles that make any view hazy and ill-defined.

The High and Over is one of those places where you can just stand and stare for an eternity. It's panoramic vista could never be captured on film. However beautiful you imagine this place, times it by ten and you will be close to the beauty that it holds.

Well, how did I do? Did my description of Alfriston and the Giant make you want to pack your bags and come and see this tiny corner of the world I call home? Did you get an urge to rush down to your travel agent, grab him by the throat, throw your hard earned cash at him, and demand the next flight to England? If you have just woken up from forty winks and found this book resting on your lap, keep it to yourself I'll be round to fix your sewing machine later!

This picture was taken at my in-law's Ruby wedding anniversary. Sarah, my daughter is pulling a face because she hates having her picture taken. Sarah is responsible for several of the pictures in this book.

The Bluebell Woods at Lions Wood with Yana and Rolly. Before the bluebells flower the woods are carpeted with white wood anemone. Rolly always looks at me as if I am mad when I make her pose for a picture. They say it takes over 600 years for bluebells to carpet the ground like this. A sure sign of an ancient woodland is well established bluebells.

Alfriston Market Square with the market cross just visible and Queen Victoria's Chestnut tree. The Smugglers Inn is just at the far right of the picture.

More wonderful open downland with endless miles of tracks and paths to roam.

Nelly and her Daffs

Spring was in the air and Easter just around the corner. The year was spinning out of control and Christmas was just a distant blur. The bright, tough little daffodils were out and braving the high winds that were bashing England. Plants that had lain dormant in the cold soil and silently monitored the passing of winter, were awakening. When the time was right they would rush forward with a surge of energy. Like a young teenager with a rash of hormones.

I had called on a regular customer and, while we were talking about the spring flowers, she reminded me of her mother who used to look after the church flowers for a village called Ninfield.

In Ninfield, a small rural village in the heart of East Sussex, there is a sweet church called St Mary's. It was built in the 13th century, a couple of hundred years after the Norman invasion. That's when nasty Normans came, beat up the locals and built much of the magnificent architecture in our country. Then, a few hundred years later they took the Stena Line ferry back to France for some more baguettes and Brie. The pretty church has a fantastic feature inside, a *musician's or minstrel's* gallery high up in the roof. It was added in the time of King Charles I, and you can only get to it by ladder. This means every time they had a service, the musicians would have to clamber up the ladder, passing up all their musical instruments. I would love to have been at one of the old services to have seen them in action.

Outside the church, just around the corner on *The Green* almost on the main road, are the village stocks – made of iron from one of the many old foundries in the area. This is where the local troublemakers would have spent their weekends after getting drunk or causing an affray. The most popular time to lock up a disturber of the peace in the stocks, was on market day. On that day you would be shackled up and totally humiliated by village youngsters, often having old rotten vegetables thrown at you. I bet that would work wonders with some of our young hooligans today.

Nelly Simmons was the woman who looked after the flowers at the church for 60 years. In springtime, as Easter drew close she would keep a close eye on the daffodils – or *lent lilies*. They had to be just right for the Easter Service. In all the years that Nelly looked after the church flowers she said that the daffodils never got it right. They were either too early or too late. Often she would round up the village boys and make them all rush out and pick the daffodils. Then keep them warm to bring the blossoms out, just right for the special day. What a sight the church must have been, all bright and beautiful for Easter.

Nelly was not one to be messed with. She was a local girl who was born only a few miles up the road in Herstmonceux. When flowers needed picking for the church she would grab anyone to help her. She even accosted the choirboys during their singing practice. One spring, when snow was in the air and there was a possibility that the flowers would be damaged, she rushed into the church, stopped the vicar and choirboys in mid song, then dragged them out and made them run up and down the village banks, picking the wild flowers. Nelly was one of the colourful village girls that had carried on the same practice that many had done for centuries before her.

One of Nelly's favourite flower arrangements for the Easter Service was a cross, made of wild primroses. Primroses still grow in profusion along the old, twisty lanes around Ninfield and they made a beautiful display in St Mary's, all along the aisles.

Can you just see it now? A lovely old church with bright spring sunshine pouring through the stained glass windows throwing a rainbow of colours onto the church floor. The whole village, lined up along ancient wooden pews, singing hymns. The vicar standing before his flock, singing his heart out, leading the choir in rejoicing – and all around are Nelly's beautiful wild flowers. Ah, how spring really is the time of rebirth! What a great time to be alive. Spring just fills you so full of hope. When things in this world are sometimes so bad and frightening; something as simple as a bank of daffodils can fill you up with enthusiasm and hope for the future.

Nelly said goodbye to this world on her 96th birthday. For her service, the whole village picked the wild flowers for the church. Her service was said to be the most beautiful anyone at the church could remember. Her ashes were scattered in her garden where, they say, she still tends to her flowers.

When Nelly would pick the wild flowers she would say to people. "They are God's flowers and they are going to God's house."

I just thought I would share this little story with you as the sun is shining and spring bursting out all over. At Ninfield the banks are full of the flowers that Nelly picked for St Mary's. She would have been proud of their display this year, as they look a picture. Mind you they are way too early, so she would be telling those daffodils that they have got it wrong again.

The Whipping Post and Village Stocks at Ninfield. Made of iron at one of the many foundries in this area. It has lasted for many centuries. I expect the local hooligans of today would think twice if they were locked in the stocks on market day.

Eastbourne Road in spring. No other flower on the planet sums up more delight than a host of bright daffs in spring.

NBG

"You've got a snowballs chance in hell of fixing that," the man grunted over his cornflakes. "I've seen more life in a tramp's vest." I looked down at him as I neared the table saying nothing. "Only called you cause the wife made me. See I am an engineer and if I can't fix it then it's NBG – *no bloody good*, ye' see."

I felt my blood rise to the challenge!

"Well I will have a quick look anyway just in case, you never know there might be some life left in the old machine."
"Pah, waste of time I tell yer, waste of time, two weeks I been lookin' at it and it still ain't working." A few cornflakes followed his last statement out of his mouth landing on the table in front of him. He picked up the largest one, examined it, then put it back in his mouth and continued munching away.

I was up to the challenge. First of all I checked out all the scratched screw-heads, which gave me a clue as to where *the engineer* had been on the machine. Once I had seen where he had been messing, I examined the mechanism and started to put back all the parts that had been removed. Out of the corner of my eye I noticed him eyeing me up as he leaned, like a possessive bear, over his breakfast bowl.

"Ah, I see the problem," I announced with a touch more enthusiasm than was needed, just to rub it in a bit. "Simple really, all I need to do is adjust the top shaft a smidgen and the machine will be fine." I went about my work with a smug smile as he grunted, burped then noisily unfolded his copy of *The Daily Sport*. He slumped back in his chair, turning the tabloid pages from picture to picture, occasionally peering over the top corner of the paper to watch my progress.

Within 20 minutes I had the machine purring away, much to the annoyance of the old bugger who had been joined by his wife. She made the matter worse by letting him know how useless he was for not being able to fix the machine. If he had not been such a totally unpleasant human being I might have felt slightly sorry for him. As it was, my soft nature was soon to be rewarded with a wallop.

When I asked the couple for £25, in perfect unison they both went into choking fits. The man's face contorted into a spasm of pain, as if he had received a heavy blow to the groin, from my toolbox. *The sights you see when you haven't got a gun* I thought to myself.

"What do you mean £25, you have only been here half a bleedin hour!" spurted out the man.
"Yes, but."
"But nothing." He interrupted quickly, "I ain't made of money."

I could have mentioned the fact that I was in a house worth at least a quarter of a million pounds or told him how I could not fail to notice the Jaguar on the drive outside, but I kept to my professional patter that had served me well over the years.

"Mr Watson, you are paying me for my expertise, skill and experience, not to mention coming to your home. You picked up the phone, I have done everything else, surely you are pleased to get the machine running well are you not?"

There was a moments indecision as the wife nodded but he shook his head. I could see a split appearing as she was pleased to have the machine working even if the husband had to cough up a bit of cash. *Ah! divide and conquer*, I thought.

"That ain't the point boy, the money is, and it's too much!"
"Look Mr Watson, I have driven all…"
"Save it for the preacher." He interjected pulling a large wad of folding money out of his back pocket. He counted out the notes and flung them across the table. "Bloody rip-off if you ask me." He said it in such a way that I was in no doubt it was the end of the discussion.

I took that as my exit cue and decided to follow it out. I noticed his wife was looking quite pleased with herself, standing half-hidden behind her man. She was probably enjoying the whole show.

I grabbed all my tools and headed for the door, happy to get away from the house just as quickly as I could. At the door I was almost pushed over the threshold, there was a bang right behind my ear as the door slammed shut. I laughed to myself. This was not the first time and it would certainly not be the last time that I would embarrass a husband, fixing the "unfixable" machine. A terrible urge swept over me to bend down and shout through the letterbox, "Have a nice day!" Instead, I jumped into the car and headed towards my next call, smiling all the way. There are just some things in life that give great satisfaction and pulling a big-head down a notch or two is one.

I was looking forward to my next call. Vic, the husband of my customer, is from the old-times, he is stuck in a time-warp from a forgotten era. He had no time for airs and graces, with Vic you got what you saw, a ruddy-faced countryman who could be as rough as a wild pig and as gentle as a new born lamb. He has the biggest nose I have ever seen, it glows like an iron pulled fresh from the blacksmiths forge. His wide face was always bright and cheerful with a thousand tiny veins that spread like spiders webs across his ample cheeks. Vic's smile would brighten up the most miserable of days. It was really more of a cheeky grin wrapped with sinful thoughts. When he laughed, which he did often and with much vigour, he revealed a mouthful of broken teeth reminiscent of a city skyline at night. Vic's hair was his *pièce-de-résistance*. It was grey and long with wavy white flecks and always untidy. Vic kept his unruly hair swept back over his large head, like an aged musketeer. His hair suited his nature, reminding me of a wild day at sea, when waves have whipped up into turmoil with white caps riding on the tips.

You could not help but like Vic. Each time I went to fix his wife's Italian Necchi machine he had me in stitches. Not so much by what he said but by what he got up to. Going to see Vic was like visiting a wicked uncle who taught you everything that your parents told you never to do.

I drove along the small country lane towards Jevington and his cottage. The skyline that had been bare to the stars all winter was now starting to fill with greenery from the sprouting trees that line so many of our country lanes. The great horse chestnut tree that slumbers peacefully until April before awakening was just coming to life. Like a lumbering giant rising from a heavy rest, the chestnut stretches out his limbs and unfurls his huge green fingers to bask in the spring sunlight. By the end of April all beneath his sweeping canopy will lay in shadow, only the bluebells glad for his shade. Within days of raising each of his green-fingered hands would open like parasols and hold up bright candlesticks of white blossom to shake at the wind as it rushes by. Each candlestick heralds the promise of deep bronze conkers in late autumn. Each conker held tight, protected by a small spiky green sea mine that has pricked many a child's eager finger as they prise out their champion conkers. Schoolyards of old across the width and breath of England once resounded to the cheer of the conker championships. A prize conker, held with a fraying shoelace was every schoolboys dream.

Of all the great British trees, only the beech and maple are inclined to sleep longer into the year. The fresh beach leaves are as soft as the down on an Icelandic goose. You could stuff a pillow full of the downy green leaves and a young princess would sleep as soundly as if cradled in Aphrodite's arms.

I pulled up alongside the waist-high Sussex-flint wall of Vic's cottage. As I was getting the toolbox out of the back of the Land Rover I glanced sideways, over the short-flint wall towards Vic's rear garden. It was his pride and joy. This is where he grew his prize onions for the village fayre, where he forced his rhubarb in the early part of the year to give it a head start and where his gold award dahlias took many a prize at the years annual flower show. Vic's garden-allotment was his life. He had told me many years before something that I will always remember –

"If you want to be happy for a day, get pie-eyed (drunk).
If you want to be happy for a week, get hitched (married).
If you want to be happy forever, get a garden."

Never a truer word has been spoken and I totally agree with Vic's sentiment about the garden. There is something so pleasurable about working the soil that it should almost be banned. Anyway I digress and we need to get back to Vic. I glanced over the wall towards his large allotment that ran for a hundred yards from his back door down to the neighbour's fence. There sitting in the middle of a row of freshly dug earth is Vic. Not too unusual you may think. But hang on a mo. Vic has pulled off his braces that hold up his over-large trousers that normally rest just below his chest. He has pulled down his old Y-front pants and is sitting with his bare backside in the middle of his allotment, he had a wry sort of pleasurable smile creeping over his face as if he was testing a fine wine. Vic saw me and shouted out.

"Hello Alec. Come for the wife's machine 'ave we, I won't be a mo." I looked away embarrassed at having caught him obviously doing something that would get him arrested in town. He saw my efforts to avoid looking at him and laughed. "Don't be shy now, I ain't got nothing you ain't seen somewhere before." *You may be right* I thought, but I did not want to be personally introduced.

"What on earth are you doing Vic?" I said as Vic struggled to his feet and roughly brushed of his backside before making himself presentable again. "Arh you may well ask Sonny Jim, and now I am going to tell you how the old folk in times long past did things in the country. You see the land is like a book, all you need to do is know how to read it."

I walked along with my tool box to the gate just as Vic hobbled over to hold it open for me. He untied the gate latch, which must have been broken for a dozen or more years, and held it ajar. "It's like this you see my boy," he started, resting his hand aimlessly on my shoulders as we walked along the cottage path up towards his back door. "Back in olden times it was always important to know when to plant your first row of seeds. Well, while your brain may not know when that time was, your bum does."

He laughed out loud as he saw my bemused face. "It's what me father did and his father before him and every sod in my family since Adam was a boy. Come the time of year to put in the first crop we would go down to some freshly dug soil, drop our pants and stick our bums firmly in the soil. If it made our eyes water then we didn't put anything that needed to grow in the ground as it wasn't a-ready. But if our rosy cheeks slumped into the earth and the ground was warm and soft to your bum, then planting time was here. Now how simple is that, eh boy? You caught me just enjoying the moment, so to speak"
"Vic you constantly amaze me, I think I could learn more about the country from you than any book could ever teach me."
"Well that little test is as true today as it was a thousand years ago and it will be the same in a thousand years to come. Come on in now, lad, and I'll get the pot on for a nice brew."

Vic had a shine in his eye that had not diminished during his 87 years on this earth. I had heard that he still risked a slap, pinching the barmaids' bums down at the Eight Bells pub. You could take a black and white photo of Vic and it would be almost impossible to tell which era he came from. Every time I saw him he wore the same clothes. Big baggy, brown-cord trousers with braces holding them high up over his round belly. His shirtsleeves always rolled up past the elbow, as if he was ready for anything and a tie. Whatever Vic did, he wore a tie. I suspected that tie did not come off even for a bath, which, I had the feeling, he only took in spring and autumn. I adored Vic and his wife, they just seemed so happy minding their own business and letting the world turn. They were always busy. To this day Vic boasts of only having one holiday in his working life and that was a weekend in Blackpool, for his honeymoon. "Hard work never did me no harm," he would always say when moaning about the lazy kids of today.

Vic filled up his old kettle and slung it over the cooker. "Marge won't be long now. Take the weight off your feet while your waiting," he said pulling a rough, heavy oak chair out from beneath the kitchen table for me.
"Well Vic, you told me all about your rather unorthodox soil test but did not tell me if the soil is ready for planting, is it?"
"Won't be long now boy another week I should reckon if the weather holds."
"Marge will be back any mo now. She has been down the Market with her eggs."
"She still sells her eggs then?"
"Oh wild horses could not stop her sellin' them. Got the habit during the Blitz back in '41. Her mum kept a couple of dozen layin' hens in the back garden and she would supply a few for her family an' the like. All above board like, she would have to fill in a daily chart for some government inspector that turned up every blue moon, jus' te' see she wasn't sellin' them on the sly like, what with rationin,' coupons and all. Every month one of the hens went for the pot, but Marge could never eat the boiler, she went 'ungry on those nights, bless her little cotton socks. Funny thing that about chickens you know, chickens will eat jus' about anythin' you chuck down for `em, the only problem is the mess they make."
"And the noise the cock makes at four in the morning." I said
"Pah, you *townies* know nothing today. If you want to stop a cock from crowing you do not let it stretch its neck. It cannot crow until it's neck is fully extended. So, if you do not want it to crow before a certain time in the

morning just keep it in a run where it cannot lift up its head, then let it out when you like."

"It is so easy when you know the answer eh Vic?" I said smiling.

"You are right there boy, the question is always easy when you know the answer."

I sat chatting away to old Vic passing time in idle gossip, putting the world to rights until I heard the gate squeak. "That'll be the old girl now." Vic chirped up with a happy smile. "Now don't go lettin' on about my bum in the dirt or she'll give me-a-slappin',' mum's the word, ye-hear." I nodded wondering who would believe me anyway.

I spent another hour in the happy company of two of my favourite locals from the old country, servicing Marge's machine for her and listening to Vic's pearls of wisdom that slipped so easily from his crooked old mouth. Marge was one of my regulars, she sewed so much that I called on her at least twice a year, sometimes more when problems happened on her machine. She made just about every stitch of clothing that she and Vic wore. Plus everything else from the tablecloth to her peg bag. The pair had devoted their life to one of near self-sufficiency as could be possible in these times. Vic had just the one suit. Marge had let it out three times over the years as his ample belly expanded with age. "One suit is all you need in life boy, and it will be coming with me when I move on from this world."

Vic was one for the stories and, when Marge was out of the way, he would let slip of his old poaching days when no pheasant or trout was safe in East Sussex. He actually taught me a lot of useless information that may come in handy when we workers rebel against the gentry and the revolution begins. I loved getting up to no good when I was younger and many of his tales of after-dark romps in the woods, around some of the fine houses of the area, rang true with me. However, those tales are for another day.

As I left, Vic saw me off down the path. Once again, Vic put his hand on my shoulders as we walked to the back of the Land Rover with my tools. "Thanks for that me boy, you're a scholar and a gentleman," Vic said with a wry old smile. He was always clever like that. One of Vic's talents was that he made you feel good. He dropped one more of his pearls of wisdom on me as I turned to go. "Listen ere' Alec, I'll tell you one more thing that me father told me. *You can judge the character of a man by how he treats someone that is of no use to him.* Think about that boy, never a truer word has left my lips."

I drove down the lane from his cottage, right by the chickens that had provided Marge with her eggs for the market. I was sorry to leave. I could have happily stayed all day and let time slip away. How right Vic was, that simple but profound statement is one of the surest tests of human nature you will ever get.

Vic's knowledge of the forgotten arts of farming were magnificent, and his field craft undeniable. But what I will never forget about Vic was the sight of him sitting with his old cords pulled down to his knees and his bum in the soil. It was that priceless look, a look of pure, lustful pleasure on his old crinkled face as he made a mental note of the soil's temperature with his own, very unique, temperature gauge – his pimply-wrinkly backside.

Vic's pig in the apple orchard. She knows she should not be there – it is written all over her face. Vic keeps his pig in a stye not far from his cottage, but she escapes regularly in the autumn to pinch apples and bears a striking resemblance to her owner.

CAPTURE THE MOMENT

It had been a quiet week for work, what with the Queen's Golden Jubilee and the start of World Cup football. England had beaten our old arch rivals, Argentina, 1 – 0. It was the first time England had won against them since 1966. An estimated five million people took time off work to watch the match.

There has been an unexpected national outpouring of patriotism in England. With the new independence and devolution of power that Labour has brought about England, Scotland, Northern Ireland and Wales have all gone their own ways and for the first time people are showing it. The white flag with the red-cross of St George, has popped up like mushrooms on a warm autumn night. By the millions, they are fluttering from every post and pillar, car and washing line in the country.

Several factors have all come together to bring about this euphoric surge. Inflation is low, the economy is on a 40 year high, people have money in the bank and a job. Unemployment is the lowest since 1949 with only a few hundred thousand unemployed out of the 60 million inhabitants. There has been a huge influx of asylum seekers, they have poured into England by the thousands, risking everything for the possibility to have a chance for what we all take for granted. This has made English people more aware of their own birthright. Then we have had the wonderful celebrations of Queen Elizabeth and football madness, as England beats one opponent after the other, on their way to the quarterfinals. Bring all this together in early summer of warm days and short nights with plenty of time for boozing and barbecues and there you have it – a country in celebration. A mixture of circumstances has brought about a unique feeling of being English and being in England in this moment in time.

It has been a real pleasure to watch and be part of something that I never thought I would see in my lifetime. It is as if the young and old of England have rediscovered a common ground, one which they can all participate in. People have come together like never before and are really enjoying the moment.

Because of all the celebrations, little sewing was being done and by Saturday morning, I had cleared all my calls and was looking for something to do. The weather was warm and wet. Our spring this year had lasted three months with dry and sunny, cold and wet all shoulder to shoulder. We have had a lovely April so the blossom has developed into a superb fruit crop that only needed a few weeks of sunshine to give us a bountiful harvest. I looked out of the window and wondered if it was worth the risk of going for a short walk. Rolly must have read my mind for all of a sudden she was by my side whimpering. Yes, a walk it was. Even if it was just around the block.

Although it was late spring/early summer, the weather had been its usual wet self, just warmer as we marched closer to summer. There had been just a few days of sun in the whole of May, and June was starting just the same! Maybe that is why British people so reflect the weather. I have found that on a bright spring day everyone is in a good mood. I met a lovely old Sussex girl once who told me *there is no such thing in Sussex as bad weather, you're just wearing the wrong clothes!* Remembering that, I decided to wrap up well. Noting another old Sussex proverb *never take your second vest off until June is out.* Wrapped up well against the elements, Rolly and I set off along the streets in an aimless amble.

Walking is such a great thing to do. It allows you to think at your leisure and ponder. You can put everything into some sort of order when you are alone with your thoughts.

I wandered by St Marys church at the top of our road and saw all the fresh confetti stuck to the damp pavement. The spring weddings in England are such lovely events. At St Mary's they have a super choir and a good set of bell-ringers so you really get the whole shooting match there. Rolly was concentrating on all the pavement smells and before long, we were at the foot of the Downs. It was a split decision, go up onto the Downs – a long and arduous walk heading up some 500 feet – or turn back.

I stood at the entrance to Chalk Farm and pondered for a second. The weather had not got any worse and there was only the lightest of winds. With enthusiastic encouragement from the mutt, we headed for the hills.

We walked past the farm and headed out along the footpath that cuts below the Downs. All the spring lambs had gone. Farmer Brown would have shipped them off to the markets at Hailsham and beyond. The market at Rye that had been used for centuries by all the farming folk with their regular livestock markets, had lost part of its livestock licence. The prime development site had been under attack for years but valiantly resisted all development efforts. Unfortunately, *Foot and Mouth* had been the cause of new government legislation. This new legislation was financially, and practically, unworkable in Rye. I just have the feeling that although the market still does well the death knell had been rung for Rye Market.

I could not help wondering how many other rural markets would be heading the same way. In the last twenty years over half of our entire village shops in England have disappeared followed closely behind by the post offices. Now it is the turn of the markets. It is a sad fate for a time-honoured tradition of the village market.

The whole of our country actually developed around the market place. The way England looks with all its towns and villages is a direct result of markets. Like lifelines, they connect to each other across the country. When bartering was a way of life, the market was the life-blood of the community.

How different now when we just pop down to the local stores and pick up weird and wonderful produce from the four corners of the world – kiwi fruit from New Zealand and pineapples from Hawaii. It was not that long ago that we all looked forward to our local grocers having the first of the season's tomatoes or cucumbers. Now we eat plums, pears and peaches all year round and think nothing of it.

The lower field at the base of the Downs was full of dark brown cattle that were lying in the wet meadow, casually munching like we would a sandwich in front of the TV. The grass was vibrant green, still in its flush of growth before seeding.

Instead of walking around the base of the Downs, I headed diagonally upwards, towards the public footpath that leads up to *The Saddle* at the top of Butts Brow. It was a long slow climb, Rolly eagerly pulling. The smells of the pavement had transformed to the smell of open land and the possibility of Rolly's favourite thing to chase – rabbits. She has never caught one but that never stops her trying. If she did she would not have a clue what to do with it. The mutt is scared of my cats, so a wild rabbit would be a real mouthful, so to speak.

It was a slow, heaving climb up the steep slopes. I followed the narrow track of cow's hoof-treads that gave me some leverage on the wet grass. My feet were soon covered in a sticky mess of chalk and grass. In Sussex, we call this sticky mud *loving mud* as it clings to you so well.

I stopped about halfway up for a breather. I was heaving hard, long breaths from the heavy climb. My lungs were filled with rich Downland scents that poured out of every flower and plant, a smell as sweet as nectar. I had not noticed but, as I climbed, the weather had closed in all around me. I turned to look down at the flatlands and shires of East Sussex that would normally lie before me. There was nothing. I was alone in a milky cloud of silence on the steep hillside.

All was still and quiet. The mist had stolen away the sounds of the day. The busy traffic I had walked by, half-an-hour back, had disappeared into a thick coat of silence. My heart was thumping hard, beating blood around my perspiring body. I walked on and upwards, each foot clinging for grip.

I had learnt many years ago not to wear heavy-soled walking boots in the Sussex mud. They soon filled and became like lead weights on each foot. Instead, I wore light, leather, trainers well rubbed with Vaseline. About a hundred feet below the summit, I circled the edge of the old disused chalk pit. Chalk used as much by the Romans two millennia ago as we do today, for the perfect building material. I was now in the low clouds. The heavy mist had drenched me from the outside. I pulled on my woolly hat and zipped-up my coat. Inside I was damp with perspiration. My muddy shoes were soaked – as were my trousers, right up to my knees from the long wet grass.

I reached the summit and stopped for another break. The bonfire that had been lit to celebrate The Golden Jubilee had burnt a big black patch on the grass. I had seen the fire, *the beacon*, glowing bright in the night sky during the celebrations. It must have been a great effort to move such a large amount of old wood and broken pallets up here and then to clean it all up afterwards.

Crawling up a blade of grass was a ladybird with the lucky seven spots. The Sussex name for a ladybird is a *Bishop Barnaby* (probably because of the red cape). I picked it up and let it crawl up my palm. I slowly turned my hand as it clambered over the fine hairs on the back of my hand towards my middle finger. *Bishop Barnaby* stopped for a quick drink from a droplet of water that had collected in the tiny trough where my fingernail sinks under the skin. I stared at the little beast as it cleaned itself off, raised its cup like shells, like a gull-winged sports car then hovered away into the mist.

There is an old Sussex rhyme about *Bishop Barnaby* that young girls would ask if they came across a ladybird. They would hold it in their palm and ask –

Oh Bishop, Bishop Barnaby,
Tell me when my wedding shall be.
If soon comes my special day,
Open your wings and fly away.

There was no sound, no other sign of human life. I was up in the clouds. Lost in time. The Downs had taken on a strange and unfamiliar appearance, low pressure had dropped the sky down onto the land. A slight breeze rose up on the ridge and nudged the all-enveloping mist. The wind sent the mist whispering over the Downland, through the sharp-tongued thistles and soft yellow buttercups, over the bright, happy daisies and around the waning cowslips. It hit my hot face with a welcome washing of cool, fine spray. I closed my eyes and breathed deeply, absorbing the entrancing scene – straight out of a Bronte novel.

Some may think it mad to be out on such a day! I was in heaven. I was warm, wet, happy and exhausted all-in one. Energy is a funny thing. It can desert you so quickly when you are doing something that you do not want to do and yet, at other times, fill you with endless stamina.

It is all down to stress, positive and negative. Negative stress is one of the biggest killers we all face in our lives. It can be caused by anything. We even cause it ourselves. There are a hundred names that stress hides under, *chronic fatigue syndrome*, depression, constant exhaustion, anxiety, and ME are some. They are all close relations of stress. Even having a good day

is a real bonus. I find that having one whole, good day is rare, rare indeed. We have good moments during a day but rarely a whole day.

For example, a few years back, that wonderful, bouncy, Italian jockey, Frankie Dettori, won seven horse races on one day. That day will probably dominate the rest of his life, impossible to repeat. Frankie rode his horses to victory on a wave of enthusiasm. He was wound-up with enough positive stress to allow him to achieve the unachievable. However, when he got home the same evening, he found himself in a terrible mood. He had the best time of his life but it did not last one whole day!

We worry about things that we have no control over. We worry about stupid little things that have no bearing on our lives. We all do it, exhaust ourselves needlessly! For example, experts tell us that worrying too much about dying, on average, can reduce your life by up to 10 years. Amazing, ironic and true. However, I find that you have to capture the good moments in a day and really enjoy them. For, as sure as a fox chases the rabbit, those good moments soon pass. The person who first said *Carpe Deum* or *seize the day* really knew what they were talking about. If there was one guiding rule to follow it was surely that, I would just change it to *seize the moment*.

This was one-of-those moments. Standing on a damp hillside, lost in mist and time, one of those special all-for yourself moments that fill you with a surge of positive energy and a lust for life. I was as happy as a pig that had snuck into the vegetable patch while the family were at church.

After a while, I called to Rolly. She appeared out of the mist, eagerly wagging her tail with a soaking wet muzzle where she had been foraging in the damp grass, her bright eyes and panting breath told me how happy she was. We headed downwards, moving along a semi-circular footpath that cut, like a horseshoe, around the huge hollow known as *Tascombe*. I watched every step along the steep path. One slip and I would have tumbled down several hundred feet ending unceremoniously, in Farmer Brown's field. The cattle that lived on the Downs had made the going hard on the descent, their heavy hoofs leaving awkward shaped tracks in the slimy, chalky, mud.

I slowly dropped down below the clouds. I was aching and glad to be using different muscles to the ones that had been used to get me up the hillside.

As I reached the halfway point down the hill, the distinct *cawing* sound of a crow floated up to me from the coppice below. It broke into the silence of the day, *caw, caw, caw,* then hush once more. I stopped by a seat that was placed at a beautiful vantage spot. Normally it would overlook endless miles of open landscape, of towns and villages stretching as far as the eye could see.

Today there was just the hazy outline of a few houses in Willingdon. The rest of the world lay unseen in the all-engulfing mist. I could just make out the steeple of St Mary's Church, with its chestnut tiles, and the roof of the excellent Wheatsheaf Pub that stands on the corner of Church Street. Over the years, many a traveller, coming off the Downs would have enjoyed a hearty meal and the rich ale at the Wheatsheaf.

Rolly chased some magpies or *Devil's children*, as country folk would call them, off the barbed-wire fence as I climbed over a stile and down onto Butts Lane. I had one last look back up the path that I had trodden. I could see my lonely footprints disappearing up into the mist.

I crossed the slippery road and made my way down towards civilisation. Wild clematis stretched across the small path seeking new footholds on which to continue its journey. Clematis that in autumn, would have hoary seeds and called affectionately as *old man's beard*.

I was presented with the first sign of human life. A sign spat out – **Private Property – Trespassers will be prosecuted**. Yes, I was definitely back among the human race.

I got home and threw all my sodden clothes into the washing machine. I ran upstairs, chasing Rolly into the bathroom. I gave her a good scrubbing in the bath, with Tom's *Africa* shower gel. She smelt lovely when she leapt out of the bath. She shook water everywhere and ran off in disgust. I am sure she much prefers being smelly.

Some warm clothes and a good cup of tea was all I needed. I looked out of the window at what appeared to be such a miserable day. How misleading it looked – for a wonderful host of experiences was waiting for anyone brave enough to explore outside. Yes, I thought, what a good idea it was to go for a walk, just to capture that *special moment*.

I'VE MET 'EM ALL

I have met them all I was thinking as I drove away from my last customer. She used to hand-sew real hair into the front bands of *syrup of figs* – wigs. The job would take two weeks of painstaking work on each wig and cost the customer hundreds of pounds.

Yes, I had met them all; rug makers, belt makers, harness makers and sadlers, horse blanket makers, net makers, blind and body warmer sewers, curtain and carpet sewers. Makers of settees, seats, sofas, lingerie, linen and lawnmower covers. Drapers and dressmakers.

I had met upholsterers that sewed up bus seats, car seats and covers for toilet seats. I had met people who covered bricks for doorstops, ripcord for parachutes, car wheel covers, glass cases and also soft-top car-hood repairers. The list went on and on, cobblers, corset makers and cereal-bag sewers. Sail makers, pillow stuffers and lace makers.

Rosette-ribbon makers, coverers of beer barrels, champagne cooler makers, balloon manufacturers. Embroiderers and para-gliders, coffin makers and drapers. From bridesmaids' outfits to baby clothes, lifejackets to loincloths, I had visited them all. Thousands of trades all using the humble sewing machine to ply their trade.

I was playing, in my mind, with the trades that I had come across over the years when *white van man* came hurtling towards me down a narrow country lane. I swung the Land Rover hard against the embankment as the van bore down on me. I closed my eyes as it screeched past. There was a bang and the noise of shattering of glass. I opened my eyes and saw the remains of his wing mirror scattering over the road.

"Yeeha," I cried in sheer delight at *white van man* getting a bit of well-deserved payback.

I had no damage at all, my wing mirror had just swung around. However, it was a short-lived delight. As I looked in my rear-view mirror I saw a horrible sight. *White van man* was attempting to turn his vehicle around in the narrow lane. It was like déjà-vu. *White van man* had chased me before, many years ago, and now it was all happening again.

I put my foot to the floor and shot off down the lane. I dropped left at the first junction, then right at the crossroads and hit the main road. I slipped into the traffic and sped away. I had just started to relax when I spotted the white van coming down the road in the opposite direction, the remains of his wing mirror dangling from the side door. He must have shot straight across the last crossroads and missed me. I knew there was no way he could turn round in the traffic. As he saw me I gave the red-faced *twerp* a polite smile and wave. He gave me a furious two-fingered salute. What a laugh I had, it made my morning.

I made my way down to Hastings where John Logie Baird stayed in 1923. Whilst convalescing from a serious illness in Hastings he was so enthused by the healing properties of the seaside resort that he continued his pioneering work on the vacuum tube and transmitting pictures. And so it was that in the little seaside resort of Hastings the first television images were born.

****

I was off to the Old Town in Hastings and my next customer in All Saints Street. As I dropped down into the town I passed the house where Joy had lived. I met her a few years ago when she was a frail 86 years old.

When Joy was a girl of 12 her pride and joy was a Singer model 15k treadle. She kept it in her bedroom and would save her pocket money to buy material for dresses.

When Joy had enough money saved from her chores she would rush down to her local haberdashery and buy material for a dress or blouse. She would then wander up the main street and see what everyone was wearing. She would peer into shop windows for ideas and designs. Then she would rush home and make something. She was such a proficient machinist that she could buy the material in the morning and wear the finished garment to supper.

Her Singer was her pride and joy. Her grandmother had left her two gifts. One was the Singer treadle the other was sewing lessons. One day she came home from school and rushed up to her bedroom. Her treadle was gone.

Her father had sold the machine to pay for food and coal. He tried to explain to her but she was still heart broken. Her father had run up large debts. Later they had to move home as well.

At 15, Joy got her first job. She saved for two years and on her 17th birthday she bought a second hand Singer 15k treadle from a pawnbroker. She rolled the treadle home and made a dress on it the same day. She then wore it to her birthday party. It was the proudest day of her life.

I was called out to replace the old leather belt on the machine and give it a good service as the machine was to be left to her granddaughter and she wanted it to be perfect. She had spent many years teaching the girl how to use the treadle. The youngster loves the Singer and has made her first blouse on it. She has called the Singer *Joy*, after her Nan. She told me that when she uses the treadle she can feel her grandmother by her side.

****

What a delight on the eyes Hastings old town is, for anyone who adores old buildings. Tackleway, George Street, the High Street and All Saints Street have a mixture of buildings that would satisfy any historian, architectural lover or enthusiastic tourist. You can wander down the narrow lanes where some of the ancient houses lean out over the streets. Old wooden-beamed, and new smart town-houses all mingle together into a delightful concoction to feast upon.

My customer Ethel, had a Brother Compal Galaxy. The computer machine talks to you and tells you when you have done something wrong.

"You have not put your buttonhole lever down, do not proceed," came the voice from inside the computer as I tried to sew on it.
"Really," I replied, "and what if I do not want to do a button hole, eh?"
The computer was silent – so smart and yet so stupid all at once. "It is a common fault Ethel," I said as I stood up and turned to her. "It won't take me long to sort it out."
"Well done Alex! Rosemary at the fabric shop told me you were the one to fix it, *'If anyone can, Alex can'*."
"I am glad to see Rosemary is still singing my praises. I shall miss her when her shop closes. I think the whole of the Hastings area will miss her too."

"You are right there Alex. Her haberdashery is the best in the area. One spoon or two?" Ethel was holding a spoonful of sugar above my cup of tea waiting inquiringly for my answer.

"Just the one Ethel. I am cutting down so I can fit into my old trousers again."

"I know the feeling Alex, it comes to us all when you only have to sniff a cake and it leaps onto your hips for life."

We both laughed and I went about resetting the faulty *talking machine*.

How true it was. Months of cutting down on my goodies had produced a slow slimming effect, but also a constant hunger that every now and again had to be satisfied to stop me becoming suicidal. Beachy Head was far too close for comfort I could leave a note on the cliff top, *not enough cake!* That would confuse everyone. I finished up at Ethel's and made my way back to the car.

I walked by the *Stag Inn* and a welcome aroma drifted out from the kitchens. Time, I thought, for lunch!

"I'll have your best fish'n'chips please." I heard myself saying.

I had hypnotically walked into the pub and sat myself down, browsed the extensive menu, from a rack of ribs to Hastings fish pie and placed my order. The pub, built in the 16th century is rich in character. Low-slung oak beams and open fireplaces fill the pub with a hospitable feeling.

Above the fireplace are the mummified remains of two cats. They sound a bit gruesome but great age has mellowed them to no more than an interesting curiosity. During the *great plague*, a form of bubonic plague that coincidentally died away after the *great fire* of London in 1666, it was supposed that possessed cats brought the plague. People did not realise that it was the fleas on the rats but they were right in suspecting cats. There were two particular cats in the area that belonged to Hanna Clarke. She was reported to have been a local witch and her cats possessed by the devil. Her cats were caught and mummified in the chimney. Well, that's the story anyway.

As I tucked into my fish'n'chips an old couple came into the pub and sat behind me. "What shall we have dear?" asked the man.

"I am going to have the steak and kidney pie," replied the woman.

"Well, I will have the scampi," the man said. He got up and walked to the bar to order his meal. When he got to the bar the man turned to his wife and shouted over, "What are you having dear?"

"Pork chop and apple sauce," she replied.

"And what did I want?"

"You wanted the fish pie dear."

The man ordered the meal and came and sat down again. "What did I order dear?" he said as he got to his seat.

"The scampi dear."

I was totally confused at the happy couple and it showed on my face as I was ordering a half pint of *Bishops Finger*.

"They have been coming here every week for a long time," the pretty serving girl said, nodding towards the old couple. "They have terrible short-term memories! Talk to them about the war, they will tell you the day that they enlisted, ask them about something five minutes ago and they are blank. They are as happy as larks in themselves, just no short-term memory."

I went and sat down again, smiling at the couple as I got to my seat. I went back to tucking into my feast. Their lunch arrived. "Now who is having the pork and who is having the fish pie?"

They looked at each other and the lady said, "You are having the pork chop dear, the fish is mine."

"Are you sure love?" the husband enquired.

"Of course I am sure, I have not lost all my *lemon drops* yet." She replied sweetly.

I sat in silence, supping my beer and soaking up the ambience of the pub as they tucked into their lovely meals like children. Scoffing the lot in very quick time. I had only half-eaten my meal before they were finished.

As they got up to leave the lady called over the bar, "See you next week." The barmaid replied, smiled and waved farewell. As they got to the door, the old man looked at his wife and asked, "What did you have for lunch dear?"

"I am not sure," she said. "But it was lovely. I am already looking forward to our visit here next week."

Cricket on the Saffrons pitch with Eastbourne Town Hall and church spires behind.

The Green Man at Ringmer. A wonderful country pub. Notice the two local girls!

Ladies Day at Ascot: with our neighbour Jane, daughter Sarah in the middle and Cathy, one of our good friends.

The Horse and Groom at Rushlake Green on a busy afternoon. There is nothing like a lovely pub lunch in the country.

Herstmonceux Medieval Festival. The festival makes a great day out with jousting, archery, battle re-enactments and a host of other activities including roast boar and apple sandwiches.

The Stag Inn in the Old Town of Hastings.
Hastings Old Town has some of the finest architecture in our area.

*Brightling Beacon, one of the high points in East Sussex that is not on The Downs.
A spectacular view of the Sussex Weald is seen from this point.*

*Firle Place – home of the Gage family for centuries. The Georgian house is set into the beautiful
downland near Firle. It is the epitome of a grand country house.*

Arundel Castle in West Sussex. Ok, so West Sussex is a bit out of my area but the castle – home of the Norfolk family – is one of the finest in the land. If you closed your eyes you could just imagine the Sheriff of Nottingham waving his fist at Robin Hood from the battlements.

The Towner Art Gallery in Old Town Eastbourne. Once owned by the Towner family, it is now in a poor state of repair. On the edge of Gildredge Park, it is one of the grand old houses of Eastbourne.

The Rye Windmill, looking simply majestic. Once this windmill would have been essential to the bakers of Rye, now she just sits silent.

The village Post Office at Crowhurst near Hastings. All these old post offices are under threat of closure. It will be a great shame if they all go.

THE GOLDEN JUBILEE

To mark 50 years on the throne, Queen Elizabeth II, celebrated with a party. A party to end all parties. It was a *world* party. Now I am going to get a bit mushy about our sovereign so hold on to your hats and I will try and describe the sights, sounds and emotions of a unique occasion **The Queen's Golden Jubilee**.

The noble and proud figurehead of the oldest *continuous* democracy in the world, the Queen, threw a big *bash* to mark her 50 years on the throne. It was an amazing occasion – only three other monarchs in the whole of British history have ever lasted longer. The Queen put on four days of celebrations. I do not think I have ever seen anything like it and probably never will again. I was really pleased that the weather had been good. Mind you, in some corners of our *sceptred isle* it was pouring down, still in the usual British *stiff-upper-lip-style* they put on a brave face.

At one street party the rain did not stop the celebrations. A soaking wet man, dressed from head to toe in red white and blue, simply said…
"It does not matter that it's raining because we are British."
He held up a pint of beer and saluted the Queen. His spirit was how we all felt. Mind you, I think the whole world knows how eccentric we Brits can be.

The start of the four day celebration was on 1 June 2002. It was a very special day. It had been 50 years before when a beautiful young princess awoke to the news that her father had died and that she was Queen of England.

Elizabeth had been on holiday at *Treetops Safari Ranch* in Kenya at the time. This year, to mark the occasion, some 2002 beacons were lit across the world, from New Zealand to the Artic Circle, one fire being at Treetops. All along the south coast of Britain, the old warning beacons were lit on all the high places.

Beacons were originally put on the tops of hills to notify us of approaching danger or as signals for other events. Can you imagine communications today relying on a fire on top of a hill to warn you of danger? Imagine the beacon-keeper having to light the fire on a damp and stormy night, high up on an open hillside, with invaders approaching. Not a job for the faint hearted. If the French were invading or the Spanish were coming up the channel the beacons were the fastest way to send a message to the ports and London. Now we would just pick up the phone or better still check out CNN and find out what time the armada were leaving port.

They say that in 1588 Queen Elizabeth was at the races when she heard the news that the Spanish King had sent his armada to invade England. Luckily, the Duke of Tavistock, good old Sir Francis Drake, finished his bowls at Plymouth and gave them a good spanking. For this years' celebrations, once again, both the beacons at Firle and just up the top of our road at Butts Brow were lit in the evening. Queen Elizabeth herself, at The Palace, lit up the last of the beacons.

It was a long and happy weekend for us. On the first day of the celebrations, our noisy resident pigeons woke me, just before 4 am in the morning. The two overfed males were leaping around the roof and sliding down the tiles, play-fighting. I peeked out of the window to see a bright sun already well up in the sky. By 4.30 I was in the garden, still in my dressing gown, cup of tea in one hand a pair of secateurs in the other. Early mornings are such a great time, it's really the wildlife that makes it so special. They seem to have their big surge of energy before we humans even open our eyes. I remember being so thrilled that the weather was going to be good in the south-east of the country. All the really big celebrations were taking place in London with the centre of events being at Buckingham Palace and St Paul's cathedral.

Our wonderful monarch had managed, sometimes with great difficulty, to keep the Royal Family together. She had seen 10 of her Prime Ministers come and go, from Winston Churchill to Tony Blair – no, he has not quite gone, yet. She had seen a world change beyond all recognition. From the austere, war-torn and rationed 1950s to today, where the Commonwealth has become a huge family of nations all across the globe.

During the four days of celebrations, the Queen had some mind-boggling festivities and processions prepared. How a 76 year old woman has that sort of stamina I shall never know. She worked tirelessly throughout the four days, with Prince Philip, her stalwart, always by her side.

My favourite part of the celebrations was a huge rock concert at Buckingham Palace. I was not invited to the palace but 12,000 other lucky peoples names were drawn out of a hat to attend. We all entered a big competition where our name was just picked at random, so I could have been there. However, I enjoyed the event on TV. It was broadcast live to over 60 countries and 200 million people. There were two nights of music, one on Saturday for classical lovers and another for popular, rock and you-name-it music.

Although all the anti's were out predicting a poor response to the Queen's celebrations they got it completely wrong. The doubters and moaners did not get it a bit wrong. **They got it completely wrong... big time**! A combination of World Cup football and Royal fever had swept across the country and it was a real pleasure to witness. I have never seen so many rows of bunting and flags, hanging from every possible vantage point. A wave of patriotic fervour had swept our green and pleasant land. Yes, *God save the Queen* was on all our lips as we showed our Queen and our country that we are proud to be British!

Predicted figures for the turn-out in the Mall, in London, during the concert were 50,000 to 100,000. Well over a million people turned up and the next day it went *bananas* for the procession to St Paul's. Over two million people crowded the streets. Can you imagine a million or more voices singing as one? You could probably have heard it in space.

The wild party that Queen Elizabeth had at her *pad* took your breath away. It had a line-up of stars that will never be matched. I will run off a few that I can remember. I had better start with Kermit, what a little green frog was doing there talking to Ruby Wax was anybody's guess. The party got under way with Brian May from *Queen* standing on the roof of Buckingham Palace, alone, with his electric guitar. He played *God Save the Queen* in his own inimitable style to rapturous applause. Then there was that great silky tongued old crooner Tony Bennett, the weird Ozzy Osborne who luckily, controlled himself and did not bite any bat's heads off on-stage. Then there was the masterful Eric Clapton and that wonderful, gravelly-voiced, Joe Cocker.

The list was endless as one after another, great performers came onto the stage and entertained us. Annie Lennox sang with such passion that we all felt exhausted by the time she finished. The hilarious comedian, Lenny Henry, made the best joke of the evening. He was trying to show how much United Kingdom as a nation, had changed over the last few decades, especially towards racism. He is a great topical comic and spotted a black guardsman on guard outside the Palace as he arrived for the concert. His joke went something like this.

"Things have changed a lot in the last few years," he said. "I spotted a black guard on the way in tonight." He paused as the crowd wondered what he meant and then continued. "Isn't it nice to see a black man outside The Palace with a gun and nobody's arresting him?" – Even the Queen laughed.

There was S-Club 7 with their final song together before the group split. Phil Collins beat the drums with electric energy – his hands had to be bandaged after the show – and Tom Jones sang *You can leave your hat on* that wonderful song from that oh so British film *The Full Monty*. Ricky Martin oozed on stage as Atomic Kitten purred. Even our own Eastbourne group Toploader performed. Emma Bunton from The Spice Girls was excellent and The Corrs, well their name sums them up, you watch them and just think, cor! Shirley Bassey looked beautiful and ageless and belted out a song in her own, priceless way. Queen, the band, played and Ben Elton made us laugh. Mis-Teeq sounded like angels and looked just as good.

The list just goes on, Blue sang and Brian Adams with his broken wrist came on and played. I think he summed up the performers commitment to the event and to the Royal Household.

The Beach Boys' Brian Wilson was certainly having *Good Vibrations*, Ray Davies from the Kinks was there and so was Rod Stewart. His fabulous and unique sound could only be copied by mixing up a cement mixer full of gravel and sugar! The list was endless as hours of non-stop music entertained the huge crowds that had gathered outside the Palace and all the way down The Mall. There was Steve Winwood and Sir Paul McCartney. *All you need is Love* echoed around the world and electrified the crowds. The super talented Sir Cliff Richard entertained us all with his endless ability. Elton John sat alone at one of the impressive pianos inside the Palace and knocked out a beauty. Dame Edna had us all in stitches with her funny anecdotes.

To finish off, a million pounds, and some three tons, of breathtaking fireworks blasted into the night sky above The Palace, with Robbie Williams' *Let Me Entertain You* hammering out of hundreds of speakers.

No one has ever seen a turn-out like it. It took everyone by surprise, partly because we all started to believe the cynics who continually hound the Royal Family, saying the monarchy was an out-of-touch and outdated relic. From the staggering reception the Queen and her family received, it looks like a republic is a long way off.

240 years ago George III commissioned the incredibly ornate *Gold State Coach*. It is like something out of a fairy-tale, no better, even Cinderella never went to the ball in a four-ton coach of glittering gold, pulled by a team of eight beautiful horses with four postillions. The procession was a colourful pageant of our rich heritage. The Queen travelled the three-mile route to St Paul's amidst a throng of well-wishers shouting and cheering her as she went by.

At one point, when the Queen's procession arrived at St Paul's, the roads were just awash with hundreds of thousands of spectators. They were waving tens of thousands of flags, some wore the large flags like capes around their shoulders. The noise was deafening as countless people whistled and cheered – swept away with the mood of the moment.

In the weak sunlight of the day the scene, a mass of heaving and celebrating humanity looked like a surge of multicoloured water, a human tidal wave, rushing down The Strand. Brilliant, just brilliant! And the crowds! Well, they were so well-behaved that in the four days of celebrations there were just four arrests.

After the London parties, street cleaners cleared up over 50,000 empty champagne bottles and 75 tons of rubbish. Now that's what you call a party! Oh what a celebration! Oh what a show! Pomp and pageantry at its best.

At St Paul's, the Archbishop of Canterbury Dr George Carey, made a magnificent speech. I cannot remember his exact words as I heard them but they were close to this. The Queen looked close to tears as the Archbishop spoke. *"She had bestowed upon her the heavy burden of which*

she did not seek and accepted the responsibility of Monarch with all her heart. – We find this enduring vision woven through the fabric of your reign like a golden thread. Your majesty Elizabeth, you have the respect and affection of your people. You do indeed reign with our love."

The Queen's Jubilee Celebrations were organised and overseen by Sir Michael Parker. He must have been very proud of all the people that put so much into it. From the Caribbean street processions, which were risqué to say the least to the Hell's Angels on motorbikes roaring up The Mall. They even had a procession of flower-pot men from the 1960s TV show *Bill and Ben*, then there was the always perfect *Queens Guards* and military processions. This summer it really was the greatest show on earth.

On June 3rd the day's celebrations were started with a 41-gun royal salute in The Royal Park. That was the signal for all the street parties to begin across the country.

Street parties and village celebrations were organised in every corner of the land. Flags and bunting were strewn everywhere. It was a real pleasure to see and feel a nation, once more, finding something in which they could be proud, something in which they could all join in together. Almost every town and village throughout my whole area had celebrations. Even people that were not involved in a street party or a bash at the village hall invited friends and family around to watch the whole thing on TV, to join in with the celebrations that were happening everywhere.

The small villages had parties but even large towns like Eastbourne had a mass of celebrations. A huge party continued all day along the seafront, with events and bands playing at *The Bandstand* culminating in a spectacular fireworks display off the end of Eastbourne Pier. There was dancing and music from 10 in the morning until 11 at night. The Riverboys, a local and very talented group played at The Bandstand while fireworks exploded into the night out at sea. It was a sight to revel in and enjoy, to soak up the atmosphere, to be *one amongst the many*. There are very few occasions in one's life where everyone comes together to join in one celebration. It was like a thousand birthdays all on the same day.

While it may have been impossible to recapture the community feeling that people often referred to in **The good old days**, those days of post-war *togetherness*. We certainly managed to embody the mood of a nation happy with its monarch.

Some villages in my area, including Cuckfield and Barcombe, closed the entire main road for their celebrations. Tough luck for any travellers wishing to get to Lewes. They had to take a huge detour. Even the tiny village of Ripe closed off its main street for a big party outside the village stores and pub. In Barcombe they had beer races where you raced up and down the street and at the end you had to down a pint of ale – half a pint for the lasses. Any of the contestants unable to drink the beer had to pour it all over themselves instead.

In Newick they had a scarecrow competition. All contestants taking part built a scarecrow out of anything handy. I think around 100 scarecrows turned up for the judging. There was one still strung up on a building as I went to work the following Wednesday. At The Cuckmere Valley celebrations, they roasted meat on spits over open fires to feed the throng of villagers.

In Coombe Martin in North Devon the celebration tables stretched for two miles and in Birmingham over 25000 people joined in one party. Of course the Irish outdid us all and in Ballymena Co. Antrim they had a non-stop four day party. In Potton, Bedfordshire, the Queen gave special permission for a Jubilee beer to be bottled bearing her picture.

The final procession by the Queen led back from St Paul's to Buckingham Palace where she witnessed the unveiling of a wonderful hanging appliqué made by the Royal School of Needlework. The school was founded in 1872 by one of Queen Victoria's children. Among many things, they are responsible for the upkeep of the Royal robes and tapestries. The huge appliqué, took 12 members of RSN 1500 hours, over four months to complete. Zoe Patching, one of my customers' daughter's was one of the 12 who were responsible for embroidering and compiling the finished product. Embroidered emblems from all over the Commonwealth, were sent from each member country, and attached by the RSN. Two Commonwealth symbols were placed at the top corners, one of which was sewn by Zoe. The emblems were framed by a wreath of golden roses and looked simply magnificent. After the Jubilee the appliqué was sent to hang in the *Commonwealth Institute*.

The Commonwealth's last tribute to the Queen was a fly-past over The Mall, by Concorde, which though old, is still the pride of British aviation. The nine Hawk jets that make up *The Red Arrows* accompanied the supersonic jet. With *Land of Hope and Glory* blazing and the crowd whistling and cheering they roared overhead, streamers of smoke in red white and blue trailing behind. It was a stirring, patriotic finale to four days of great celebrations.

Finally, the Queen and her family waved goodbye from the balcony at The Palace and went inside for a well-earned rest. One last emotional wave to her adoring public from the window and she was gone. She had worked tirelessly and held a smile for four continuous days. She had laughed and cried with us as we revelled in the majesty and the spectacle that had taken place.

One of the highlights that I will always remember, was when Prince Charles made a speech at the pop concert and referred to The Queen as *Mummy*. It was so funny when he said it, and sort of sums up our feelings towards her. She just gave him a knowing glance as if to tell him *not to go too far*. If I could have one wish it would have been for The Queen Mother to be there. The Queen Mum really enjoyed such great occasions. I can still see her now, always in blue, a light veil over her face, dropping down from the brim of *another new* blue hat and that special way she had of waving to the crowds. Well, it was more like stirring clouds than waving.

All in all, Britain and the Commonwealth came together in a mass celebration and outpouring of affection for our monarch. We had celebrated with pomp and pageantry, in a unique British style and put on a show that few will ever witness again. It will be something that children talk about all their lives. As one young girl said, "It was the most fantastic day of my life."

Although Queen Elizabeth is a constitutional monarch with little real power, she has used her superb business mind and positive charm to keep the monarchy in harmony with parliament for half a century. In her Guildhall speech she said one line that sums up her feelings, " I am so proud of you all."

Though we may not realise it, everyday we have a great deal to be proud of. Our Queen symbolises and embodies the soul of everything that is *great* about *Great Britain*, and nobody can ever deny she throws a great party!

A 2002 Golden Jubilee Eastbourne Street Party. This scene would have changed little from 1953 to 2002 – any excuse for a good party!
(With kind permission of Becketts Newspapers.)

The 56th Signal Squadron Corps Band marching from St. Mary's Church, Old Town to the Town Hall. The Lamb Inn is one of the oldest in the country and a great place for lunch.
(With kind permission of Becketts Newspapers.)

The gold State Coach used by the Royal family since its commission by George III over 240 years ago. Queen Elizabeth used this coach for her Golden Jubilee.

The Village Shop at Upper Dicker.
The Village Shop is the lifeblood of any small village and still a pretty sight.

The beautiful church of St. Mary's in Church Street, Willingdon.
This church, at the top of my road, rings its bells every Thursday night. The church where both our children were christened holds a soft spot in my heart.

Eastbourne Pier at dawn. In the far distance is a huge crane that is turning over a barge that capsized off the coast while bringing rocks to Eastbourne.

Chapel Hill, off Cliffe High Street, Lewes. Chapel Hill is a steep climb, but the views at the top over Lewes are superb.

Eastbourne Town Hall. Eastbourne's most impressive Victorian building – a delight to behold.

A thatcher hard at work along our street. Thatcher's use Norfolk reed for their long life and durability. It is an age old art that continues to this day.

The Buccaneer, a superb character-filled pub next to the Eastbourne theatres. Often frequented by the acting profession.

Me at Beachy Head with an Arabian Salker Falcon. There are native Perigrine Falcons nesting on the downland but they are rare.

BARMY BUSTER

Out of all the animals that I meet on my rounds none compare with Buster. Buster is a middle aged British bulldog. His character has been formed by his experiences. For example, if a golden retriever comes into his line of sight he will go scampering off and hide. That is because, when he was a young, frisky male in his full bloom of life, he made an amorous approach towards a retriever. She bit him on the snout so hard that, to this day, he wheezes. When Buster breathes, he sounds like an Italian espresso coffee machine under a full head of steam.

Buster thinks he is human. He knows this as surely as he knows that cats, all cats, are fair game, to be chased down and hunted at every opportunity. Buster bears a startling resemblance to Winston Churchill. All he needs to make this picture perfect is a cigar and a smoking jacket. Every time I meet Buster he is getting himself into hot water. Like the time he swallowed one of his owner's golf balls and had to undergo emergency surgery to retrieve it. Or the time when he rescued a tiny starling from the neighbour's ginger tom. Once it was rescued from the jaws of death, Buster brought it into the kitchen and sat, watching guard over it, until his owner found it. Because of all his mad antics his owners nicknamed him *Barmy Buster*.

On the day of my last visit to the house, *Barmy Buster* was in supreme form. He had been relegated to the kitchen as he was making a nuisance of himself and I was unable to get on with my work. He had taken to grabbing my screwdriver and running away with it. To make up for his banishment to the kitchen, Buster slumped down onto the floor and pushed his nose down into the crack below the kitchen door. I suppose he thought it was the next best thing to actually being in the same room as us. I could not help but laugh at the sight, or rather the wheezing noise that Buster was making under the door. He would snuffle in and out with his extraordinary, totally unique, hissing sound. As much as I tried to concentrate on my work I kept looking towards the door and the sound Buster was making.

Pam, his owner, and I were talking about her mother's old hand machine when I happened to glance over at Buster wheezing. I noticed a small spider scampering along the polished wood floor, right towards Buster's nose. It is funny how the smallest of things can sometimes catch your attention. I was watching the spider out of the corner of my eye as I carried on talking to Pam. Sure enough, the spider walked right by Buster's wheezing nostril.

Suddenly the spider disappeared, sucked up by Buster's nose. There was a split second silence and then Buster erupted. From the kitchen came a howling and yelping. Pam dropped her drink and ran for the kitchen door. She flung the door open to find Buster in the middle of a manic dance. In his enthusiasm to keep in touch with what he was missing in the living-room Buster had inadvertently sucked the spider straight up his one good nostril. In the kitchen, he was doing a mad dance of the *whirling dervishes* as he ran manically about scratching his nose and snuffling like a crazed boar.

As Buster saw the kitchen door open he made a mad dash to escape and ran straight upstairs. Followed closely by his bewildered owner.

"He sucked a spider up his nose," I shouted as Pam went by.

Then, as Pam went up the stairs, Buster came hurtling down. Pam turned and rushed down. Buster rushed back up. I looked on in amazement. Only Buster! I thought, the one dog in the world that could suck a live spider up his nostril.

The pantomime went on for several minutes, with Pam screaming at Buster, and Buster not paying the slightest bit of attention as he ran madly about the house knocking everything everywhere. Eventually, like an old wind-up record player running out of power, Buster dropped exhausted to the living-room floor. I grabbed my surgical torch that I use for examination of the internals of my sewing machines and a pair of *Swiss* precision tweezers.

"Do you think that you could hold Buster still enough for me to have a look and see if I can spot the spider?"
"I'll have a go," she panted. "He won't bite you. Just see if you can remove the bloody thing before he gets his energy back."

With Pam lying breathless over Buster, I dropped to my knees and dived in.

As I leaned over his panting head, Buster's hot, stinky, dog-breath was making my eyes water. It was not until I got really close that I realised just how big he was. His head was probably bigger than mine. He was panting on his side, his huge pink tongue was lying, dribbling onto the carpet, like an enormous, slimy, pink squid that had slipped out of a bucket. I carefully folded back the skin around Buster's nostril and shone the torch down it. Sure enough, half way along his one good nostril, covered in horrible slime, was the remains of a spider. It looked like Buster had been successful in his frantic efforts to kill it.

I gingerly reached in to remove the spider as Pam whispered calming words into his ear. My hand was shaking like a leaf. I had removed a million items from countless cavities in endless sewing machines, but never a spider from a mad dog's nose. On my third attempt, the tweezers emerged with the slimy body of a dead spider. I smiled triumphantly as I turned the tweezers slowly in front of Pam's face.

"So, that was what all the fuss was about!" Pam sighed.

Buster looked up at me and gave an exhausted whimper of approval.

I wiped my tweezers clean while Pam rushed out and filled a bowl of water for Buster. She stroked him lovingly while he slurped away. Within a few moments Buster looked no worse for wear and had his usual glint back in his eye. He then returned to his wheezing. Pam slapped him on the backside and banished him to the garden. Buster turned and sulked off to find a sunny spot where he could recover from his ordeal. Pam and I cleaned up some of the mess in the living room that now resembled an earthquake.

Pam then put the kettle on while I soaked up the remains of her spilt coffee from the dining room floor.

"Now you have seen first-hand why we call him *Barmy Buster*. You have to see him in action to believe it." Pam said, returning and handing me a drink. "All's well that ends well," I chirped up. Secretly having enjoyed the whole show.

LETTER TO MUM

Dear Mum

I do hope that you had a nice day at work, at home it has been just awful.

I am not sure how the cat got into the washing machine but she sure looks nice now that the glue has gone. She seems to have enjoyed the wash, when I let her out she was so happy she ran all around the house even up the curtains. She has found a nice new place to stay in the back of the cupboard in the spare bedroom.

A ghost has left muddy footprints all the way from the garden to the fridge, I chased him off but not before he stole all the cheese and crackers. I know uncle Wedgwood won't be too pleased about the broken vase in the hall but he might be impressed with how I stuck some of it back together.

How the goldfish managed to leap out of its bowl is anybodies guess, I was way too busy but sucking it up with the vacuum cleaner worked like a dream and does not seem to have harmed it. I like the way it swims on its back now and he looks quite cool with those large eyes. The dog escaped just after you left and if Wispy does turn up, the missing part of his tail is in the top drawer in the kitchen.

I thought I should let you relax when you got home so I have gone to discover Africa, my friend has told me that it is down behind the supermarket off the High Street. If you feel like talking to me at some time in the future I will be at Nan's.

Love

Your favourite son

XXXX

CAN'T SAVE 'EM ALL

Summer arrived suddenly and, as with most British summers, would probably disappear just as quickly. It arrived just in time to coincide with the start of Eastbourne Tennis Week.

Anna Kournikova would be stirring up the young blood around the town. My son Tom's friends describe her very simply as *fit*. I suppose when you are 16 that is all you need to say. Anna is officially the most beautiful woman in the world – a title that is short-lived. Martina Navratilova was making a welcome appearance after nine year's absence from the Eastbourne grass. Once the warm-up at Eastbourne is over, war begins in earnest on Centre Court at Wimbledon.

At Wimbledon, the grass will have been manicured and pampered to perfection and the strawberries and cream stalls will be ready for the consumption of the 3,0000 kilos of strawberries normally consumed by eager Wimbledon enthusiasts.

The temperature had shot from a poor 9 Centigrade on Friday to a sweltering 29 in two days. The soil that was sodden from months of rain warmed and oozed a new and wonderful scent, the scent of summer. Flowers, that had been waiting patiently, suddenly opened their petals to the sun and threw their scent to the four winds. Cherries that had hung, stone-hard, in the leafy shade showed their first hint of pink, like the blush of a schoolboy after his first kiss. Yes, summer was definitely here and there would be a few old Sussex folk deciding that they would not have to wear two vests for a few weeks.

Monday arrived with a bang, a desperate phone call came from a distraught machinist that had to make the wings for *Chitty Chitty Bang Bang*, the new London musical spectacular that was costing six-and-a-half million pounds. It was to be the most expensive musical ever staged with Michael Ball and Brian Blessed in the key roles. I selected a suitable machine for her husband to pick up and kept my fingers crossed that the cars wings would not fall off during the first performance.

I was glad to get away from the phone and before long I was merrily meandering along the country lanes towards Alfriston and my first call of the morning. I only had two calls all the morning so things were going to be a breeze. Well, so I thought.

The grasses were waist high and swayed, rolling with the warm breeze. The fields flowed with the wind in great waves, moving like herds of invisible beasts stampeding across the countryside. The lack of cattle from BSE and Foot and Mouth meant there was little need for the farmers to cut the grass for feed. It would have been a good year for silage with at least two good cuts being possible. Still that is life and we could do no more than get over the problems and carry on. Farmers were restocking with fresh animals and before long the trials and tribulations of the previous year would be just bad memories, then once more the fields would be cropped for feed.

Crows were squabbling above the small coppices. In June their blood is up and they really go for new territory, for several days they chase wildly around the woods squawking and cawing, plucking feathers from each other. Then once the *pecking order* is established calm is restored.

I arrived at my first call just before 8 am. I pulled noisily, up the gravel driveway to *Primrose Cottage*. As I opened the back door to remove my tools a pretty young girl appeared with golden hair in corkscrew curls framing a big smile. She was dressed for school, in a bright red jumper with the school crest embroidered on it and a grey pleated skirt. "Hello, have you come to cut the grass?"

I smiled, "No, I have come to fix your Mum's sewing machine. Is she inside?"

"Yes, I shall take you to her right away, come with me." The girl reached up and grabbed my hand.

I was tugged all the way through the cottage into the kitchen. "Mum, the sewing machine man is here to fix your machine. I never knew you had a sewing machine Mum, where is it?" Her Mum stood up from the washing machine, which she had just filled. "Lucy, you are always in a rush! Just slow down, come and finish your cornflakes."

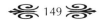

"But Mum."

"No buts! Sit down and eat up – or no games tonight."

"I am sorry," said the young Mum, wiping her hands with a kitchen towel. "You need to see my mother, not me. Follow me, it's just through here." I waved to Lucy as we went along a narrow corridor to another annex at the back of the cottage.

"Ah Mum," the woman said as we went into the main room. "There is a man here to do your sewing machine."

I looked down as I felt something nudge by me into the room. It was Lucy, smiling and wiping the remains of her cornflakes off her jumper.

"It's not me that you want dear its *Mother*." She said lowering her copy of *The Independent*.

Now I was confused! Just how many *Mothers* were living here?

"Oh, I see," said *the mum*. " Lucy, now that you seemed to have finished your breakfast in the speed of light take the man to see Nana."

"OK." She grinned grabbing me once more by the hand. "This way."

As we walked along the sprawling bungalow that stretched out like an octopus in all directions, I could not help but wonder which member of the family I was going to meet next.

We came to another room and Lucy knocked firmly on the door. A bit out of character I thought as I expected her to just barge in. "Nana," she called quietly through the door, I have a man here to see you. He is going to fix your sewing machine for you. Can we come in?"

There was a slight delay and the door slowly opened. A small lady smiled up at me.

"Come in young man, I have been expecting you."

Lucy pulled me into the room that was like a miniature house all in one room. It held just about everything that you could want to survive. "Now run along Lucy dear or you will miss the school bus."

"Do I have to Nana? You look a bit sick, I think that I should stay here today and look after you."

"No chance you little munchkin! Now you get off to school before I get the whipping stick on you."

"Don't I get a kiss Nana?"

"Kisses and kind words are earned, now be off with you."

Lucy skipped away off down the corridor giggling. "Always worth a try," she shouted back as she disappeared, her laughter trailing away with her.

"Well, good morning young man. I am glad you found us all right, we are tucked away in the middle of nowhere up here."

"Yep, you sure are! But I can usually get to out of the way places. I find I get lost in the silly places, like large housing estates. Exactly how many of you are living here?"

"Four generations, all under one roof." She replied as she pulled the cover off her Singer sewing machine.

"I have had this little beauty since my American trip in 1970, she has been my saviour for over 30 years. Now something has gone wrong with her. I do hope you can fix it as she is my best friend."

I looked at the well-worn sewing machine sitting patiently on the table for help. "Well, now that I am here we should have it all sorted shortly."

They were the words that I heard myself saying but always regretted instantly. They were the harbinger of doom! Each time I had unwittingly said those words, I would come face to face with an impossible task. This one would be made all the worse because the owner held the machine in some sort of magical esteem. She had promoted the piece of cast aluminium and plastic into an extended member of her already impressive family.

I opened my toolbox, rolled up my sleeves and got down to work. My worst fears were soon realised as the worn machine came apart. It had so much wear that I did not know where to start first. The obvious problem was it was out of time. This meant it would no longer pick-up a stitch. However, putting it back into the correct timing position was not the normal procedure. Because of the heavy wear on the parts, each time I got it right it ran for a few inches and slipped again. The main belt that runs from the top shaft to the bottom to drive the underneath of the machine was constantly slipping under pressure. I was under pressure too – because the dear had pulled her chair up to the table and was assisting me in the operation!

I had to tighten the shaft belts and re-time the machine. A job that would be much easier if I had another pair of hands. At one point, I had three screwdrivers in the top of the machine and a pair of tweezers going in from underneath. The machine was starting to look more like a hedgehog than a sewing machine.

"Well dear, she certainly is putting up a good fight isn't she?" said the old girl, sitting patiently waiting for positive news.
"Yes, I reckon I could pull out an appendix easier! This really is keyhole surgery."

I felt like giving up several times. Each time I got it right, the worn toothed-belt would slip again or another of the plastic teeth would start to break up. The belt was so worn that all adjustment had been taken up.

I stood up and stretched. I turned off the pinpoint spotlight on my forehead and prepared to tell her the bad news. Some machines are just worn-out. I could spend all day replacing old bits with new but you would still have a worn out machine. There is a point in every machine's life when enough is enough. This machine had done a good service for three decades, but its life was nearly over. Many older machines carry on, but these more modern plastic and rubber ones have a definite life-cycle and when it is over, it is over.

Yes, it would be easy to tell her. I mean it is not as if I don't tell people the same thing every week. *I just can't save them all.*

"Look Mrs Morgan it's like this."

I glanced over to her and looked into her pleading eyes. She sat at the end of the table waiting for my verdict. I saw hope in every wrinkle of her old face. I thought about how she was living with all her family – an astonishing fact in today's world where, as soon as you reach an age where you are trouble, you seem to be carted off to some home and forgotten about.

I had visited many of those forgotten people over the years and how sad each one was! I gritted my teeth and stiffened myself for the inevitable truth that had to be told. "Mrs Morgan, it's like this, you see, err – I'll just have another go and see if we can save her for you."

Well, that was not supposed to have come out! What happened to the, *you'll have to bin the machine, what do you expect after sewing on it for 30 years?* I guess I just gave in when I stared into those pleading eyes.

I sighed and got back down to work. I needed her help, which, although she was ninety if a day, I had to have. So, with her sort of shaking and pushing on a screwdriver and me juggling the other three tools at the same time, we managed to lodge a block behind the main worn belt, just enough to stop it slipping out of time. I reset the timing and gave it a run.

The smile on her face said everything! I had no idea how long the machine would last. It could have been a month or a year. It was a toss-up who would last the longest. What I did know was that there was a very happy, sweet old dear in a small annex of a sprawling cottage, sewing away on her old friend.

As I drove away I looked at my watch. I had been working flat out for over two hours on one machine. I could go through half a school classroom of machines in the same time. Mind you, I felt satisfied, as if all the hard work had been worth it. Sometimes it just takes that little bit more effort to get the reward and this was one of those times.

Because April had been glorious, inspiring a wealth of blossom from all blossoming things. The hop and apple growers were happy, as were all the vineyards in our area. Britain has nearly 400 vineyards growing some of the finest grapes for a superb range of British wines. The output is not high – it is *low yield*, as they like to put it – British wine rarely makes it out of the country. That does not mean to say that we cannot enjoy it locally as the Romans did for over four centuries while settled on our soil.

May and June had been warm and wet. So wet that we were picking wild field-mushrooms off the Downs in June, a good three months before they were due. All that seemed to be behind us now as I drove through the winding lanes towards my next call at Blackpale cottage. I drove out of Alfriston and turned right down a small lane that went over Long Bridge on the river Cuckmere.

****

I must tell you about a funny incident that happened at Long Bridge when I was a kid. In my family, I have a whole bucket-full of brothers. One Sunday we decided we would do a bit of canoeing along the River Cuckmere. We arrived and started unloading the canoes. It was one of those glorious, sunny, summer days in the Sussex Weald with skylarks singing to abandon and swans lazily gliding down the river.

While we were leaning on the gate by the river my youngest brother, Olly, had the idea that he would like to try and ride on one of the cows that were happily grazing in the field. The banks of the Cuckmere are raised to prevent flooding although not that successfully in recent years. On one of the raised ridges were several cows enjoying the rich grass growing there. We all took the opportunity to goad him on and encourage him as much as possible.

Before we knew it, Olly had leapt over the fence and was running at full speed towards an unsuspecting herbivore chewing her cud some twenty yards from the gate. For a small lad Olly made a fantastic leapfrog onto the cow's back, slapping it on the behind as he went. Olly's face, as he glanced back, was a picture. That look of complete dominance and pride – that can only come before a fall.

The peace of the warm afternoon was soon shattered as the cow leapt into life. She would have made a rodeo proud. Of course, it was only a matter of seconds before Olly's face turned from proud defiance to sheer terror! He gripped the raging beast between his thighs like a human bulldog-clip but it was to no avail. Before long, he was flying through the air in a magnificent display of flailing arms and legs.

As he came to earth with a thud in the long soft grass, we all erupted in spontaneous applause. The cow went straight back to munching grass as if she threw off naughty kids every day. Olly shook himself off, pulled up his trousers and made his way back to where we were. I must say he walked more like a man as he came towards us, as if he had risen to another level of development. He had that *wide-gait* stagger and experienced look on his face that said, *been there – done that.*

We went about our business unloading the canoes. I was the first to take the brave step of getting into my canoe as the other boys held it. Getting into a canoe is always the hardest part and in the thick undergrowth of the riverbank, it was no easy task. Just as I was nearly settled, one of my brothers shouted in alarm *Snake! Snake!* All the boys leapt back in horror leaving me to lean precariously before doing a rather poor Eskimo roll, then falling out of the upturned canoe into the muddy waters of the Cuckmere.

The boys fell about in uncontrollable laughter as I struggled out of the water rising from the muddy banks like some prehistoric mud-creature.

Eventually, after nearly half-an-hour of hard work, we were all in our canoes. We had failed to notice that, because of the low water level and the length of our craft, we could not turn about in the narrow river. Typical! The result was a one-way trip and another lot of messing around as we reversed the canoes up the river. All in all, we wasted a whole afternoon doing absolutely nothing. Mind you, isn't that what being kids is all about? Having fun and doing nothing on lazy summer days. Great memories.

These are the coastguard cottages at Cuckmere Haven.
The cottages had to be built to try and stop the smuggling that was rife for centuries. Smugglers would rush up with the flood tide to villages like Alfriston, some miles up-stream.

WILD WILLY

I must explain a little about the countryside around East Sussex and most of Great Britain. East Sussex is set out much like a large quilt. Before the coming of motorways, the country had remained unchanged for centuries. Towns and villages needed to be no more than a day's walk from each other. The reason for this are simple. If you were taking a herd of cattle, or a flock of sheep or pigs to market you needed to get them there by morning, sell them and get back before night-fall. The whole of England evolved in this way. A trip to market and back would be a few hours march each way. If you looked at a map of the country today you would see each town and village, connected by a system of roads, between, roughly, seven to fifteen miles apart. This remained unchanged until canals, railways and motorways cut through the land, changing the shape of our country that had been the same for millennia.

Another point about our wonderful country is that we are so steeped in history you can hardly put a foot down without treading on some ancient artefact or relic. The trips that I take you on around East Sussex, really only scratch the surface of what is one of the most fascinating and diverse counties in Britain. Our history is so full and mixed it is sometimes hard to see the wood for the trees.

The one dominating spectacle of East Sussex is the South Downs, almost a hundred miles of majestic, rolling downland that is visible from just about any spot in the county.

Back in the long-lost mists of time, around 100 million years ago, before man strode the earth, billions of tiny creatures were busy in the primeval seas. As they died they deposited their minuscule bodies, skeletons and shells on the bed of the warm sub-tropical sea. Eventually, over a period of some thirty million years, layer upon layer built up at a rate of about one inch every two to three thousand years, compacting down to become huge mounds and banks of soft limestone. In these swathes of limestone other creatures died and became fossilised, these fossils turn up regularly along with the occasional sharks tooth and have been given the sweet label of

Sussex Fairies. Larger softer creatures like squid and sponges perished and their bodies were left littering the limestone graveyard. They slowly dissolved away, being replaced by liquid silica that set over the millennia to become the hard stones we know as *field flints*. Sussex is famous for its flints – two kinds, sea and field flints. A flint from the sea was then modified relative to a field flint. Sea flints are smooth and polished from rolling around on the sea bed for an eternity as opposed to the field flints, which are knobbly and misshaped. Stone Age man soon discovered that both were perfect materials for weapons and much later, for buildings too. Because of this, it is easy to tell a building that has been built from local flints. Sussex, being rich in these natural resources, has become renowned for its flint buildings, barns and churches known as *Sussex Flints*.

Let's get back to the formation of our superb Downs. The rich escarpments and rolling downlands rise like a great, green, tidal wave, undulating their way through the Sussex Weald culminating in the dramatic highpoint of Beachy Head, some 550 feet (170m) above sea level. The downlands were created during the last huge building period of our planet the great deposits of limestone were heaved up out of the seas by unimaginable pressures from the centre of the earth. Nature then spent the next few million years covering the soft, white, bare chalk with soil, trees, shrubs and grasses of endless varieties.

So now you know where our beautiful and majestic downlands came from. It is hard to imagine a time when these hills did not exist, just billions of minuscule sea creatures in an endless cycle of birth and death. Still, I must posthumously thank them for their hard work, their legacy is here for all to enjoy.

The highest point around this area is Firle Beacon. It gets its name by being the high spot above Firle village. They say that, at this spot, the beacon was lit to warn of the Spanish Armada creeping up the Channel with nasty intentions towards our virgin Queen. Little good it did them. After a good whipping by Drake and some rough seas, they went home and troubled us no more. Drake, most perturbed at having to rush his game of bowls, obviously took it out on the Spaniards.

It always makes me smile when you hear old rumours, like the one of

Drake being so blasé about the Spanish attack that, when he heard the news, he simply carried on with his game of bowls. The truth is that his main fleet, based at Plymouth, could not set sail until the tide was right so he could do nothing but wait. While waiting for the tide why not finish off his game?

Up on Firle Beacon it is nearly always windy. At the top, you can let your eyes roam over the vast flatlands below. Out over our blessed county towards the High Weald in the distance. On a clear day you can see over 40 miles as the patchwork of farms and villages disappear into the haze. You can let your eyes roam in a 360-degree panorama. It is a sight that would please any human or, in fact, a visiting alien. If you wanted to show someone East Sussex, in all her glory, it would be from this spot on a clear day.

Below Firle Beacon is Firle Place. The house sits grandly in the rich and fertile farmland below the escarpment of the Downs. Firle Place is open at certain times during the year and has a wonderful display of great *old masters*, in oils and porcelain. The home of the Gage family since the 15th century, the house certainly embodies the proud feudal spirit of long-forgotten England. The building of the grand country house had reached its pinnacle by the 17th century in Britain. Buildings built during that era seem to simply exude a grandeur that has never been matched. Firle Place is a perfect example of an impressive country manor set in its own sprawling grounds. Their elegant summer Fayres are a wonderful experience. When Yana and I get the chance we dress up, me in my best Panama hat and linen jacket, Yana in a light, summer dress. Then we browse around the marquees and attractions tasting the fudge and ice creams. All low-calorie of course!

I was running way behind on my calls for the morning and desperately trying to find Blackpale cottage. I had found three *Blackpales* already but not the correct one. I knew I was in trouble when the postman sent me the wrong way! I bumped into him twenty minutes later and he apologized and sent me in the opposite direction. I had the feeling that he had no idea where he was sending me. I was getting really fed-up when I saw a farmer heaping freshly cut silage into the back of a trailer.

"Excuse me," I shouted as I pulled off the road. " I wonder if you could tell me where Blackpale cottage might be." I was shouting over the low rumble of his tractor.

"Arr now, would that be Blackpale Farm and Cottage or just Blackpale Cottage. Or maybe you are after Blackpale House or Blackpale Manor and Lodge. Then there's Blackpale Barn, or you could mean Blackpale Place. Which one might it be lad?"

No wonder the postman was confused and I was lost. I read out the address to the farmer, it did not help. But when I mentioned my customers name his face twitched with recognition. "Oh you mean Janet! I knows where she lives all right. You a Tallyman then?"

"Tallyman?"

"Door-to-door salesman."

"Oh no! I have come to fix her sewing machine, not to sell her anything."

"Surprised she's got time to see you today, what with the Fayre tomorrow an-all." He said pushing up the brim of his cap and leaning against the wheel of his tractor as if he had all the time in the world. "Now this is what you have to do lad. You see that field over there, well don't go down there as it ain't the way. You sees that large barn over there, well that ain't the way either, so I wouldn't go there if I was you. What you want to do is take the back lane down there for about ten minutes. Make sure you don't go more than 15 miles an hour or ten minutes will be too long see, as I am telling you the time by judging how long it takes me in the tractor, like. Now then, when you done your ten minutes you will see a big old oak tree, next to a wapple way."

"Wapple way?" I interrupted.

"Bridle path, don't you *townies* know nothing? Now then. Ignore that tree 'cause it ain't no use to you where you're going. When you get to the bottom of the hill you will notice an old stone bridge, lovely that bridge, used to fish for wild trout there when I was no taller than a ram's arse. More than a few times I'd take some trout home for Ma. Now go over the bridge and take the next left. Make sure you don't miss it, like, or you will end up going somewhere that you don't want to go – and no one wants to do that do they? So remember don't go down there lad."

"Great, thanks! I think I have got it!" I shouted, completely confused. I waved goodbye to the old farmer who could stretch one syllable into ten and still avoid speaking English. I started to turn the car round when he

came up to the car window. "You'll be wanting a bit of help first lad."
"What?"
"Look down at your tyre there, it's bubbling like a pot of soup over an open hearth."

I looked back at my rear tyre to see bubbles appearing through the muddy puddle that it was in.

Great! I was running late and now I am going to have to change the dirty wheel.

"You gone and run over some wire." He smirked with a knowing nod in the direction of some old barbed wire that I had just reversed over. "Not to worry lad, I'll give you a hand fixin' it. I'll just get rid of my pickling stick." With that, he threw his pitchfork into the hay and went over to his tractor and pulled the door open. His head disappeared for a few seconds and then reappeared with a big smile. "This is what you will be needin'." He said, showing me a rusty old nail about an inch long. I looked on in mixed astonishment. My mind was wondering what I was letting myself in for. The old bugger had probably escaped from one of those *care in the community* homes and was probably about to scratch his name along the side of my car with the rusty nail.

"Now roll the car forward until I signal you to stop."

Suspiciously, I rolled the car forward waiting for him to tell me to stop. I nearly hit the roof when he slapped the side of the car door. "That'll do lad." I leaned out of the car window and looked back at him leaning over my back wheel. He spat on the nail and pushed it into the bubbling tyre hole then whacked it three times with a clump of wood that was lying by the wheel. He stood up and walked back to my window. "That'll see you good for a mile or two lad, now don't go too fast or she'll spit it back out. I got over a dozen in Big Bertha over there and she's still sweet." He said pointing to his tractor.

"Thanks once again, you are a life saver." I said as I drove away wondering how many nails you could whack into a tyre before it blows up. His tractor was probably so noisy that you could hear him driving down to his local pub. He would be the one that sounded like he had snow chains on. "That will be the farmer coming now." The landlord would say pulling a pint of bitter for him. Still, he had got me on the road again and because I was running late I was grateful. Mind you, following his directions was another thing altogether!

Half-an-hour later I was parked in the shade of a large oak tree wondering if he had told me to ignore it or not. I could not face going back to ask him again. I got a headache from trying to understand his *Sussex drawl* and I certainly did not want to go further down the road that he gave me such an ominous warning about. *"You don't want to go down there lad."*

I was about to give up when I saw a woman waving to me from a small weather-boarded cottage just up the road a smidgen. I drove up to her and to my delight, found I was at the right place at last. As I got out, I examined the back tyre that looked slightly deflated but otherwise holding up well. Maybe the farmer wasn't that mad after all.

"I had almost given up hope on you, you're nearly two hours late!"
"I am so sorry, it has been one of those days when everything has gone wrong. I even had a puncture but luckily the farmer up the top of the hill fixed it with a nail."
"That will be Willy, *Wild Willy* we all call him, could talk the ears off a deaf donkey, but knows how to grow the best barley in the county. They say Willy can fix anything – badly. And mean, he is so mean he would not light your cigarette if his house was on fire"
"Well, he gave me an old nail for free, that can't be bad." I laughed.
"We have a soft spot for him really, just don't let him know." Replied Janet turning to go into the cottage.

As we entered the cottage, both ducking under a rambling rose that had clawed its way over the wooden door frame a wonderful smell hit me. The sort of smell that makes you close your eyes and smile. A smell that brings a thousand ravishing memories flooding back. It was the smell of home-made cakes.
"Wow." I said as I stood in front of a table laid out like a medieval banquet. "Is this all for me?"
"Very funny dear, they are for the Fayre tomorrow. I have tried several new recipes. I am after a prize on the jam and cake stall. Willy is one of the judges, he's a sly old sod. Before passing judgment he often sticks his fat

finger in a cake and pulls out the filling, then licks his finger with his nose in the air as if he was lord of the manor. He would not know how to use a knife and fork if his life depended on it. He would think they were only good for killing pigs."

"He did seem a bit funny to me." I said, not letting on how worried I was about going back to ask for more directions.

"Yes, I know what you mean he looks and acts as if he was one slice short of a loaf but in fact he is as sharp as a razor, it is all a put-on to get away with murder. I doubt if he has paid a penny in tax in his whole life, crafty old devil."

"When I was a child they used to tell a funny story about Willy, to point out what a sneaky person he was. I never knew if it was true but it summed him up perfectly"

"Really, do you still remember it?"

"Oh yes. It was Willy's turn to hold the raffle at the Fayre and he was supposed to supply the prize. Everyone in the village was really surprised when he put up one of his old pigs as the first prize. Well, the tickets sold fast and furious and before long he had sold out, nearly 300 tickets at a pound a piece. Then unbeknown to us, two days before the fayre, the pig died. But typical Willy he kept it quiet and on the day of the fayre still held the raffle prize draw."

"What on earth happened when the winner found out the pig had died?" I asked.

"Well, Willy gave the winner his pound back."

"Brilliant." I said "I see what you mean about sneaky, mind you," I said changing the subject, "I would give you a prize just for the smell of your cakes." "They smell simply wonderful."

It was my belly talking not my brain. A huge surge of stomach-acid had rushed up into my brain and dissolved the section that contained my willpower. It had taken control and overridden any thoughts of useless diets and calorie counting. Then replaced the vacant section with a devious gremlin whose only function in life was to prise the cakes from my unsuspecting customer. I was out of control and had to be fed. Now!

"Which ones are the new recipes?" I said staring in wide-eyed glee like a demented maniac who had just escaped his high security prison and found a chainsaw.

"Oh, those three over there are new but also I have tried a new vanilla extract mixed with Bourbon from Madagascar – in the Victoria sponge cream-filling. And before you say anything, I know that traditionally the Victoria sponge should have a homemade raspberry jam filling with no cream but I am going for the surprise tactic to sweep the judges away."

"I am pretty good at judging cakes," I said with my most professional voice. "My mother, amongst her many talents, was a Viennese pastry specialist you know."

"Really, how wonderful you may be just the person I am looking for, would you mind awfully trying a bite or two?"

Right, like I would mind!

I spent the next hour sipping tea, fixing her machine and nibbling cake samples. Boy was I happy! All I needed was someone to rush in and shoot me because this was about as good as life got! Everything else from here would be downhill.

I awarded Janet first prize for the Victoria sponge with homemade strawberry jam and butter-cream filling. It could have been used by angels to feed cupids. Second went to a wonderful, moist, ginger and lemon drizzle cake. Third to a mouth-watering date and walnut, and fourth prize was awarded jointly to a lemon, coconut and sultana cake and to a coffee sponge. Strangely enough, after being fed, the gremlin in my brain disappeared and was replaced with pangs of guilt. Only small ones though! As I left I rubbed my belly with total satisfaction and bade my farewell.

Yana would not be too angry when I told her about the relapse from my diet as I had managed to wiggle out of Janet a huge slab of Victoria sponge with the most perfect Madagascar vanilla and Bourbon butter-cream filling I had ever tasted. I drove off down the road, with a big grin on my face. Sod the slimming diet for today, I thought, as my half-flat tyre clicked away on the tarmac. How often do you bump into someone cooking cakes for the Fayre?

Now all I needed to do was figure out how to get on the judging team by tomorrow. I'll show Wild Willy who is king at getting the most filling out of a cake with a finger!

A DAY IN THE WEALD

What more could anyone ask for, I was thinking, two weeks of glorious sunshine in late June. I had no doubt that wet weather would soon be on its way. I could count the really long hot summers in my lifetime on one hand. I suppose England has to earn its title of *a green and pleasant land* somehow.

It was late morning and I had parked on a high point near Glynde having a well-earned break. I was sitting on the back of my Land Rover with my feet resting on the spare wheel with a slice of *Sussex Syrup cake* and a coffee from *Forfars* in Lewes. Oh, I know what you are thinking, *Hey, this boy is on a diet and all we keep reading is about his cakes.* Well, I have to wean myself off the stuff gradually, it's no good going through life suffering all the time. And my diet was going well. I had lost 12 lbs and, boy, was that a hard 12 lbs to lose. Yana had been wonderful trying every conceivable low-fat food ever made in her effort to help me lose weight. I cannot tell you how difficult it is to pass up on the teas and coffees I am offered along the way, with all the little extras. Anyway, back to the story. By the way the *Sussex Syrup cake* was fantastic, yum, yum, rub-me-tum.

As I happily munched away, on my elevenses, the warm breeze was showering me with the fine smells of the downland and bringing me the sounds of summer in the *Weald*. Yes, I thought, there is no doubt that the *Weald* had earned her right to be called an *area of outstanding natural beauty*. What an accolade to hold. No mean feat on this planet of ours.

Birling Gap, between Eastbourne and East Dean on the coast, is on the world's top-ten list of *most beautiful endangered places* on our planet. What a mind-boggling statistic I thought, that I live in what the rest of the world acknowledges as one of the most beautiful places on earth.

Below me, a mile or so away, the A27 was busy, as usual, with countless vehicles plying their trade on endless journeys. Swifts were picking off insects lifted high in the thermals. How different and yet – except for the sounds – how similar this view would have been a hundred years ago. Just the odd farmer's cart and the bleating of sheep. Today the gentle murmurings of the ancient countryside were interlaced with the hum of modern traffic.

I had just been to visit Irene, a sprightly 92 year-old, who was born and bred in the Weald. She had known the Sussex of old but also lived to see the new. In her lifetime she had seen a world rip itself apart and rebuild again… twice.

She had known and loved the old world. A time when lessons were learned from word-of-mouth over generations and were passed down through the family. A time when it was normal for a farmer to set a hundred traps at night to catch rabbits to sell at the market.

As a child Irene would buy fresh, wild rabbit for nine-pence each, skin them and cure the skins, then sell any spare skins to Amos Burley, the *rag-and-bone* man in Ashford Square in Eastbourne, for sixpence each. Her knowledge of curing skins would have been taught to her in the same manner and have been passed down for a thousand years.

A rabbit-skin jacket would have been the normal, warm and cosy, winter's coat and one in matched skins would have been dearly sought after and admired.

Irene had known a time when little changed for centuries. A time when the young listened to the wisdom their elders had gathered. When one's back-garden would produce food to see you safely through the year. Now, we all see the copious gardening programs on television showing how to convert your plentiful soil into a patio-infested, maintenance-free, barbecue-land.

Irene and her generation are the last of their kind. When they have gone the old world goes with them. Their knowledge will be little more than idle words in the lost pages of dusty books.

We live in a new world now. One of throw-away, where people that mend and make do are almost frowned upon. We know where the best deals are to be found in the shops and what time the *soaps* start on the box. Where shopping is now a major hobby and Sunday is spent queuing in endless shops, buying *can't live without* throw-away objects. We are in a *shop-till-you-drop* era where *disposable* is the key word. Where you can spend all day shopping then come home and turn to the shopping channel on your TV and book it to the all-expanding, super-elastic, plastic. Where an electrical store would look at you as if you were mad should you take in your toaster or iron for repair!

Teenagers watched the millennium pass wondering what all the fuss was about, while looking for their path in the world. Perfecting the ability to look bored with just about everything. This is the world where we rush at a million miles an hour just to try and make the time to have that special moment for ourselves, where we have to have our *quality time* to recover. Where we stress ourselves up and then have a *stress-busting* hobby – instead of just doing a bit of gardening.

Should anything serious happen to our modern world, it will be too late. For all the Irenes of this world will have gone and their irreplaceable knowledge gone with them.

I have been aware for some time that I am witness to this passing. A passing that will never be repeated. I am from a generation that is spanning the gap between new and old, modern and ancient. Maybe that is why I feel the need to jot it all down so that one day, someone may pick up *my* dusty, old book and relive, for a few brief moments, *tales from an old world*.

One thing that has not changed in *the Weald* is its outstanding beauty. Its ability to inspire and refresh the soul! The landscape is still a rich tapestry that has changed little since early man cleared much of the forests to plant the soil. Hedgerows planted centuries ago teem with wildlife. Originally made to mark boundaries and enclose grain-fields and stock before the invention of barbed wire. The tough, yet yielding, hawthorn and blackthorn hedges, that look like small patches of fallen clouds when they blossom, soon allowed other visitors to grow. Flora such as elder, spindle, beech, crab apple and wild clematis. The favourite of all invaders in the hedgerows was the *bramble*, one of the must-have wild fruits that we still harvest for homemade jams, wines and pies. Surely, no self respecting country house larder would be complete without a few jars of blackberry jam sitting on the shelf.

Honeysuckle crept into the hedgerows and threw their sweet scents to the breeze. Their twisting, sinewy vines so strong that they were harvested and formed into ropes by ancient man to harness their beasts of burden. Wild rose, buddleia, ash and sycamore all made their homes in this welcome new habitat.

The farmers cut their hedgerows every other year to allow them to grow wide and high enough to provide shelter for their animals against the fierce winter winds that poured over the Weald in the shortest daylight hours of the year. When a weak sun held no promise of warmth and the clear star-filled nights whispered to the frozen grasses that Jack Frost was on his way to turn the Weald into a winter wonderland of icicles and diamonds.

The wonderful Sussex Downlands are home to some of the finest sheep in the land. The Sussex lamb is wide and plump. The sheep are perfect for the rugged open Downland turf and, though not as prolific worldwide as the *easy care* Romney breed, just as hardy.

The Weald falls mainly into two parts – high and low, my area is mainly the low Weald although I often travel the roads out towards Kent that rise up into the high Weald. The high Weald hedgerows are far older with much of their irregular boundaries and hedges formed from ancient woodland. Whereas the low Weald has straighter and more defined hedgerows and boundaries, mostly created around the 18th century and at the beginning of the industrial revolution.

The landscape has not changed dramatically for centuries. East Sussex would be as recognisable today to Mr Neolithic, the first farmer, (I am sure that was his name) as it would be to Bronze Age man, whose axes felled the high and low Weald and cleared the way for their farms just a mere 4000 years ago.

The Romans would recognise this land where they grew their vines and quarried the chalk used amongst other things to make their precious quicklime for another all-important Roman building material, *quick-drying* concrete. They dragged the rich iron deposits from the Sussex soil that helped them rule the 100 million inhabitants that the Roman Empire encompassed in its heyday. In the Weald over 2000 kg of iron could be melted daily in the 70 or so forges that were scattered around the area. Over 9000 tons of wood would be needed each year to feed the furnaces of Roman Britain.

And all that just for swords and spears so they could go and stab people they never even knew. I don't know some people have no manners!

The Weald woods were an abundant resource of carefully coppiced woodlands where planting and harvesting took place on a regular rotation by the men of the forest. The very name *Weald* comes from the early Saxon for *woodland* or *forest*.

As the Romans left in the 5th and 6th centuries the scary Dark Ages began. This was the time when you had to keep an eye out for those horn-helmeted Vikings coming over the hills. They just might have run off with your wife and chopped your head off to boot! And we thought we had problems with mortgage payments.

Much of the great Roman forest of Anderida crept back over the Weald. For the next thousand years, the forests turned wild and rambling. Boar and wolf roamed in the dark places – until the arrival of an early form of the *Blast Furnace* in 1496.

Once again, the woodlands were called upon. The medieval iron industry started the first industrial revolution of the modern world. The furnaces of Ashburnham, Heathfield and Buxted roared into life. They heated the iron ore dug from the fertile soil. The huge and endless woods of oak, ash, beech and chestnut fuelled them. The product was iron that the mighty blacksmiths forged into the first iron cannon – cannon that started to build an empire that reached its zenith centuries later with the 64-year reign of Queen Victoria.

The iron industry flourished as did the people that fuelled it. Their violent history, from countless earlier invasions, had made their mixed blood resilient, strong and defiant.

Each day I visit descendants of these people, people that have grown from a rich soil and a strong history. Through these Sussex folk runs the blood of our forgotten empire. Occasionally I still come across a doorstep that has a piece of iron slag set in it. Iron slag that was once so part of the Weald that a piece of it on your doorstep was thought to bring you good luck and prosperity.

Once again woodsmen worked the Weald, supplying the wood for the building of great ships like the *Mary Rose*, with hulls and decks of oak. They fitted her with row upon row of fire-breathing dragons in bronze and wrought iron, with which Henry VIII could forge his own empire. She lived to be the prize of Henry's fleet only to sink in 1545, some 35 years after her birth. I bet that gave Henry heartburn, watching his pride and joy sink during a sea battle in *The Solent*! I would not have liked to be near him that week – chop, chop and all that.

The fleets of warships swept away much of England's great forests. The foremost of all the British trees is the Great Oak. The tree does not produce acorns until it is at least 50 years old. Hence it needs to be nurtured and encouraged. The well coppiced and harvested Weald survived. Not only survived but prospered because Weald-man knew how to nurture the woodlands and harness their fruits. This in turn gave work to many a Sussex lad with a strong arm. He could swing an axe all day long and then sip his flagon of ale, in the special seat that the respected woodsman always had in the local Inns.

In 1750, once again, English oak, better known as the *Sussex Weed* went to build our most famous warship, *HMS Victory*. It was onto *Victory's* decking that Nelson's blood dripped as he lay dying in the arms of his crew. The crew that he had just led to triumph at Trafalgar. Nelson's flagship, like all the great ships, took its toll upon the woodlands. A ship of this stature needed over two thousand tonnes of oak – 6000 trees – a forest for one ship. But what a great ship! Today she is still berthed in Portsmouth, looking resplendent, waiting silently for the call that will never come – to protect our shores once again.

England's future secure, once more *the Weald* turned to other means to survive. Around 1830 beer duty was abolished. This led to the growth of hop farms all along the south east area. Hops that flavoured and preserved the beer that the working man drank by the gallon. Bread and beer was all a man needed to give a good day's work.

So, the world turned once more and rolled into the 21st century. The iron industry had disappeared north to the coalfields. There they helped turn beautiful parts of England into an industrial melting pot known fondly, but with good reason because of the pollution, as the *Black Country*.

Chemical methods did their best to out-manoeuvre the hops industry but the Weald was not finished. Vineyards that numbered less than 40 after the last war blossomed to nearly 400 across the land – with the finest of the bunch around the Weald.

Then there was another twist. The fabulous forests and breathtaking landscapes fed the flames of a new furnace – the tourism industry.

Travellers from around the world came to see this ancient land of outstanding natural beauty that men and history had touched in their passing. Travellers from distant lands gazed at the sweeping views of the high and low Weald and the majesty of the downlands. They drove through the meandering lanes and through the English woodlands knowing that their ancestors had dug the heavy clay and chalk soils to plant their crops.

They came to see where kinfolk had felled the great trees, first with stone and antler axes, then with bronze, later with iron and then, still later, with steel axes that had edges so sharp they could fell a 100 trees and still remain keen. They came to see the Sussex folk living – in their scattered towns and villages that fitted so well into the landscape that had taken five millennia to form.

The Weald is different from the *New Forest*. That area was purposefully cleared of all villages and dwellings for mere sport. It was done to allow William I to hunt at his leisure in 30 square miles of uninhabited woodlands. He had created an artificial forest for sport, a *New Forest*. Unfortunately, his successor, William Rufus was killed by accident, hunting in the forest he had created.

Travellers came to hear that the only thing sharper than a Sussex axe was a Sussex tongue. One that could strip you bare and leave you bleeding with no more than a handful of words, or make you laugh so loud it would wake the dead that lie about the picturesque flint churches that dot the Weald, more copiously than any other place on earth.

Visitors would learn that the local's had passed down the story of the real bogeyman. As they tucked children in bed at night, they would tell of a horrible little Frenchman who was coming to get children that did not behave. They would tell stories of how Napoleon Bonaparte, nicknamed *Bony*, and later *Bogey*, would steal away bad children in the night to take them over the water and far away – never to return.

They would learn where many of their words came from, like gossip.

How for centuries the lord of the manor or the priest would find out what was being said about them in local taverns by paying strangers to drink there and listen. They paid money for them to *go-sip* ale, learn and report-back with the *gossip*.

Tourists came to hear the old folk talk about long forgotten things that were in no history books. Things like the many full moons of the year. We all know of the *Harvest Moon* in September but old folk could tell you of the *Long Moon* of December or the *Wolf Moon* in January when villagers would bolt the doors on the long cold nights as the wolves stretched their necks to the night sky. Or the worst moon of the year, the *Hunger Moon* of February when food was so scarce.

Then there was the *Crow Moon* of March when the crows scavenged the seed from the hard soil and the *Frog Moon* of April when rubbing the skin of a frog or toad on your warts would supposedly remove them. Then came the *Budding Moon* of May when the world came back to life. June saw the *Strawberry Moon* rise above fields of sweetness. And July brought the *Buck Moon* when bucks ran rampant through the forests. Often chased by a virile and handsome young king Henry VIII who enjoyed the hospitality of Bolebrook Castle in Ashdown Forest while hunting wild deer through the Ashdown Scrub and dallying with Anne Boleyn.

August brought the *Corn Moon* and September the one we all know, a favourite amongst all country folk, the large, soft, *Harvest Moon*. October saw the *Hunter's Moon* rise over many an animal that would fall prey to the tamed hawk or a poacher's snare. Prey to be salted, seasoned and stored for food in the cold months ahead. Then, once more, into winter and the *Frost Moon* of November.

Travellers came to see the small hamlets and villages, the bustling towns and seaside resorts. They came to tread in the footsteps of warriors and kings, in those of merchants and pilgrims. To walk through the thickly wooded forests and over the soft, undulating South Downs. They came to go on a journey, a journey through the Weald that would be remembered for a lifetime.

The low Weald that I gaze over today, with a cup of coffee in one hand and a cake in the other, has changed and has not changed. It has been the home to countless farmers and families throughout the ages and it has provided all their needs. How many are aware of its beauty is a question that I cannot answer.

I know that I have always been aware of it.

As a child I would roam the open lands. As a young lad I escaped from boarding school, more than once, to enjoy the freedom of the Downs, before being returned. As a teenager I sought solace in her green folds. As an adult I found that I yearned for the Weald whenever I was away. The further afield I travelled the further away became one of my great loves.

Today the perfect summer day has been one of reflection for me. One of thought and silence. Of admiration for *mother nature* and the beauty of the Weald in her summer frock. I listen to the skylark whose song mixes with the low rumble of the distant traffic and of the bumbling bumblebees. My eyes gaze over the Downs, in the distance, that lie like green sand-dunes rising from the desert with little outcrops of woodlands dotted along the fringes. Sunlight is flashing off the crows' backs as they flap around in idle play; *caw, caw, cawing* at the sky. The countryside is glowing, shimmering in the summer heat. Everything is busy. Even the clouds are busy turning the bright, green grass into deep bottle-green as they silently drift overhead in a sea of blue. The bushes are rustling in the wind, mimicking the sound of the seashore's lapping waves. And the Weald is at peace.

In the 21st century we have traffic noise mingled with skylark – and it fits!

Our modern world is still acceptable. The cabbage white butterfly is just as happy dancing on the summer breeze on her way to eat our pretty, cross-pollinated, hybrid show-flowers as she is on her way to eat wild sea kale. As the butterfly flutters-by (the original name for a butterfly was flutter-by) modern and old mingle and look beautiful together.

The rabbits that are still young and bold are playing in the fields from which the farmers have just cut the hay to fill their open barns. They are cheerfully chasing each other in small groups then stopping to nibble on the short cropped stubble.

A hare, no longer a common sight, makes a mad dash, straight through the middle of the field below me, throwing up dust behind each footfall. It stops almost halfway, stands on its back legs, lifting its large ears up to the breeze, for signs of danger, before dropping down on to its haunches and blending in with the soil. Blending so well, in fact, that it becomes invisible to my straining eyes.

Today *mother nature* is going about her business, much as she must have done since our closest star the Sun, lit up this planet, before the first human face looked upon the earth and smiled. It is almost as if the great clock, that governs all things, has stopped and time means little here.

Ancient and modern have combined, in the 21st century, to provide a feast for the senses and, once again, the Weald, a unique and irreplaceable part of England, is glowing in all her glory.

I have little doubt that, in another 1000 years, people much like me, ordinary working people, will stop and stare at this beautiful masterpiece and soak up its rejuvenating power.

Often on a sunny day I sit and contemplate on life and let the warm breeze blow me down memory lane. I look around the area in which I ran almost wild as a child. I stare at places where I know I have played but I am no longer there, the child has grown into the man. I almost expect to see myself cycling along an old road with my paper bag swung over my shoulder – or sitting on the riverbank, idly watching a float bob up and down. I see the rivers that I have fished and the trees that I climbed. I see all my life in pictures before me and, sometimes, if I listen really hard, I think I can hear the laughter of my childhood.

It was one of those glorious summer days in the Weald that you just wanted to capture and keep forever. To grab it and run off with it, like a carpet thief from a Moroccan carpet bazaar. To roll it all up, throw it over your shoulder and disappear through the crowds down a deserted back-alley. Then, when you are all alone, to unroll it and relive the magic all over again. Yes, I could be that thief. In fact, from now on, I am going to call myself by my Arab name – Shifty Kebab, or was it – Musthava Rug.

H.M.S. VICTORY

The Victory is now in dry dock at Portsmouth. She is still the most magnificent warship since Henry VIII's flagship The Mary Rose.

The deck of the Victory where Nelson was fatally wounded by a French sniper. Local legend has it that a local foundry owned by John Fuller in Heathfield forged some of the cannons that were originally on the Victory.

The back of our most famous warship.

AN ENGLISHMAN ABROAD

Have you ever seen a greener green,
Than in an English field.
Or a bluer sky than above the Sussex Weald.
Smelt air as sweet as that of home,
While foreign lands are flirtingly roam.
These thoughts and feelings spring to mind,
When my birthplace lies far behind.
As nights slip by calm and still,
With many a silent hour to kill,
It is then I think of the England I know,
And one day I will pack, turn and go,
With strength of step and heart abeat,
With eyes aglaze of thoughts so sweet,
Back from the lands which I roam,
To the Sussex Weald that I call home.

A.I.A.

FISHES AND FANCIES

"Stinks a bit down here Steve!" I shouted as we went past another tray of fish.

"Not that I noticed," replied Steve looking at me as if I had said something stupid.

"It's probably because you have worked here for so long that you are used to it?"

"Maybe," he said shrugging his shoulders which lifted his large chest-waders up and down.

We were walking through the back of *Hastings fish-market*. Well, I say walking, Steve was walking, I was picking my way around all the puddles and fish trays on tiptoe. Steve kept stopping, waiting for me and giving me that *you baby* look but it was important to try to keep clean. I have found there are three smells, that I come across in my travels, that cling to me like no other. A house with a heavy smoker will stay with me for the rest of the day. The smell of curry never leaves my clothes until they are washed and, the worst of all, fish!

I find I have to apologise for all three smells to the customers I meet down the line who give me strange looks as I waft into their homes.

Fresh fish has a wonderful smell of the sea, but it does not take long before the smell turns and lingers like no other. After a while you get used to the smell of fish. I should know – when I was a teenager I worked in a fish shop on Saturdays for over a year until I could stand it no longer. I loved selling the fresh fish and boiling up the winkles for the customers. Serving up a fillet of cod or haddock, picking out a heavy crab for a good customer and generally having fun. But the smell got to me in the end.

It was not a problem while I was at the shop. It was after. By after, I do not mean just until I got home and showered, but for about three days after. I could not help but notice the way people turned and looked at me when I walked by them. The smell lingered on and on. I tried every recipe under the sun, even rubbing mustard up and down my arms but nothing helped. You could make it worse by rubbing garlic into your hands, that disguised it for a short period but then you stank twice as bad. Did you know that if you rub enough garlic into your hands your breath smells of it the next day! True.

When I left *Beach Road fish shop*, Ken Warner, who was selling the business, offered it to me. But I could not stand the smell so I had to decline his kind offer. I got on *like a house on fire* with all of Ken's family. He was a working man who made a good living and an independent one.

I will always remember the day that I bumped into him by chance. Years had gone by since we worked together and he had heard that I had come off the work-floor and moved into a new office at the *family firm*. He called me a *traitor to the working class*! His words stuck with me for years, they had hit a nerve. I was a working man and proud of it.

As it turned out he was right and when I got back to my roots and started to earn a living once again, with my hands, it felt great. There is something quite special a working man has that no other class of worker comes close to. I suppose it is a satisfaction of actually doing something physical. I can't explain it but, like many millions of people around the world, I know it feels good.

"This is the machine Alex. It's being a right sod at the moment! It needs your special touch. I'll leave you here, just give me a shout when you are done, I'll fetch you out a nice slab of cod for your supper when you leave."

"Thanks Steve. Sounds good to me." I said as he closed the door of the net-drying hut where the big old industrial was sitting.

He left me alone to get down to work. I spent a few moments studying the inside of the hut. I had never been in one of them before. I had seen them many times from the outside on Hastings seafront. The unique style of the huts were known far and wide as they were the last of their kind in the area. The hut I was in was not one of the original, tall, slender, wooden buildings but a modern reproduction carefully built to fit in with the real ones. Inside, the huts were fitted out with multiple power-points and good lighting. It was a good job and the huts served a multitude of uses, from storage to sewing. One was even a café of sorts just for the fishermen. From the outside you could hardly tell the difference and tourists love them.

I got down to work and stripped out the corroded parts on the ailing Pfaff

triple-stitch, zigzag machine. Within the hour she was up and running and ploughing through the canvas and nylon once more. The machine had a hard life. All machines that are used for net or canvas work get a hammering. The bad news for the net machines is that you have to deal with the salt that invariably rusts the moving parts of the mechanism. Many net-making machines that I work on along the coast wear out years before their similar models do in laundries and the like.

With a heavy slab of cod in my bag I bade farewell to Steve, reminding him to keep the old Pfaff well oiled and headed for my next call of the morning. I drove with all the windows fully opened in an effort to air some of the fish smell out of my clothes. It was a waste of time as I was soon to find out.

As I drove along Hastings seafront, two priests, one Anglican the other Catholic, were carrying out the annual blessing of the sea service. Each year they perform the special service down on the beach to bless the boats and sailors that have to make their living on the sometimes perilous sea. It is probably a blessing that has been going on for centuries and with good reason. Sometimes a calm and peaceful sea can turn into a raging demon with little warning.

Amelia Cooper, my next customer, was one of my typical, sweet old ladies. She was waiting at the car park to let me in to her space and waved to me as I arrived.

"Punctual as usual Alex. I could almost set my watch by you."
"Just lucky Amelia. Sometimes I can run so late the bats are out."
"Well, today you are right on time. Now park that large car of yours in my parking bay and I will get the kettle on."
"Sure thing. I could kill a cup of coffee!"
"One cup of coffee with two sugars coming up then."
"Oh, Amelia, just the one sugar. I am on a diet," I said with a grimace.
"Silly boy, how are you going to eat the cake I bought for you if you are on a diet?"
"Cake! Well, that's different. I could murder a cake. What is it?"
"An apple Danish I know you love them."
"Oh Amelia you are going to be the death of me!" I said with a broad smile, licking my lips.

We entered Amelia's small seafront apartment that overlooked the wonderful English Channel. Although the apartment was compact, the view was made in heaven.

"I often sit here for hours staring out to sea counting all the large ships that glide by in the distance. Busiest shipping lane in the world, the English Channel, you know Alex."

"Yes, I had heard that. Mind you I can't imagine what some of the big Chinese sea ports look like. Every time I see a program on TV about places like Hong Kong it amazes me the amount of shipping. One thing I do know for sure is that there are more shipwrecks per square mile in the English Channel, than any place on earth."

"Amazing, talking of the sea Alex, you smell rather fishy!"

"Oh yes, I am so sorry! I have just been down the fish market working on Steve's machine, the *fish stink* has seeped into my clothes."

"Never mind. I have smelt worse things in my lifetime. We can eat our cakes out on the balcony, it is such a lovely day, it will be a treat. Now you get down to fixing my baby and I will get the kettle brewing."

"Sure thing boss."

The coffee and cake slipped down blissfully as I sat on Amelia's balcony admiring the view above the hum of the traffic.

"Alex, I have to go to the cash machine in town to get your money. Do you want to wait here or are you heading that way? It would be better for me if you were as I could then go shopping rather than come back here."

"My next call is at a bungalow in Bexhill. For some reason the couple have a leather patching machine they want me to fix so, yes, I can drop you off at the cash machine and you can go shopping."

"Wonderful! Let's hit the road partner."

"OK boss, let's get the wagon rolling."

All went according to plan and Amelia opened the car-park doors to let me out. I leaned over to the passenger door and opened it for her. As Amelia went to get into the Land Rover I realised just how small she was. Although she was a big girl weight-wise, she could have stood no more than five feet tall, maybe a bit less. Amelia tried to pull herself up onto the car seat but she could not do it. I jumped out and ran around to the passenger side only to be confronted by her ample posterior.

"Err – Amelia is there any way that I can help?"

"Push boy. Push!"

"Push what?" I cried in desperation. The only thing I could see was her bum, the rest of her was leaning into the car as she was grabbing onto the brake lever in a vain attempt to shift her hefty weight into the car. I had visions of the centre console being ripped out of my car.

"Push anything!"

"OK, here goes, hang on." I put my shoulder down, closed my eyes and heaved like a centre-back into the rugby scrum. This was followed by wild giggles as Amelia flapped around.

"Harder, I'm not made of glass!"

"Are you sure?" I gasped. I felt like *Atlas* holding up the weight of the world and definitely losing ground. She seemed to be slipping back out of any gap that I was not shoving.

"Of course I'm sure, I am nearly in, one more shove and we are home and dry. Put some muscle into it!"

"'Ello, 'ello, 'ello what have we here then. A kidnapping on my beat," came a loud booming voice from behind me.

I shifted my weight to see a large policeman standing by my side tapping his baton against his leg.

"Oh hello officer," I panted. "Just trying to get Amelia into the car to take her shopping."

"Amelia? Amelia Potter is that you in there?"

"It's me all right Ben. Give Alex a hand will you? I'm nearly in."

"If you say so girl! But I am not writing this up back at the station! Hang on, here she blows." A co-ordinated push between the officer and myself found a red-faced Amelia sitting proudly in the passenger seat.

"Oh it's nice up here." She said shuffling her bum on the seat. "I could get used to this."

"What's that pong?" Asked the policeman turning up his nose.

"That's just Alex! Don't mind him, he has been working in the fish market and, by the look of that packet on the back seat, he seems to have brought some fish with him."

"Well, at least there's nothing fishy going on here then! I mean that smell could have come from anywhere, eh? Ha, ha, ha," laughed Ben rocking on

his toes at his own poor joke.

"Ben, you are so rude! Now go and wash your mouth out this instant!" Amelia replied sarcastically – but with a smile.

"The only thing I'll be washing my mouth out with is a pint of beer at lunchtime," answered the policeman. "Well, if that's all you need this morning I shall carry on with my duties?"

"Thank you Ben, you arrived in the nick of time."

Ben looked at her, hesitating, to see if it was another weak joke to match his, but saw it was just her way with words.

"All in a day's work Amy." The policeman said nodding to me and touching his helmet with his baton. "All in a days work."

I hoisted up my trousers that had somehow slid down a few inches with all the shoving then ran back round to the driver's seat. With the weight that I was losing it would not be long before I needed a belt.

"Well that's one way to get into my car." I laughed to Amelia. "Thank God you are going shopping and don't need a lift back to your flat. I don't fancy getting arrested for kidnapping twice in a morning."

We both laughed and Amelia found it far easier to slide out of the car, to get my wages, than she did to climb in.

"Next time I need to go for a ride in your car I will use a stool like the Queen Mother used to." Amelia said as she waved me off down the road.

Wonderful! I thought, simply wonderful.

Within a few minutes I was stepping smartly along Acacia Avenue with my toolbox brushing against my trousers and whistling a merry little tune. I hopped across the main road and up a small street with pretty little bungalows, so typical of Bexhill-on-Sea. I was thinking that all was well in my small world. I found the address and opened the iron gate into the neat garden of well-trimmed grass and perfect flower borders. There was a small plaque on the wall with the name of the bungalow, *Betty's Boudoir*. I smiled at the name and knocked brightly on the door. The curtains to the bungalow were garish. Bright pink with white tassels. In the main window was a large lamp with a silk cloth draped over it. Pink is such a popular colour for many older women I was thinking when the door opened.

How wrong I was!

"Hello big boy what can I do for you?" Came a gruff voice.

I looked on in distress as a round man in an expensive purple, silk, dressing-gown and perfect make-up smiled at me just like a cat smiles at his prey.

I tried to smile my usual greeting but I could feel my face contort into more of a grimace. "Hi. Is this number 71?" I stuttered, I was hoping that it was the wrong house.

"Oh yes it is." Came the reply with far too much enthusiasm. "You must be Alex? We have been expecting you. Would you like me to carry your box, sweetie?" He said with a wicked smile, fluttering inch long eyelashes at me. I swallowed a slow dry swallow. "No need, I can manage it fine." Came my high-pitched reply.
"Well come in dear, don't be afraid. I don't bite you know. Follow me – Betty is dying to meet you. We have heard all about you from our Peacehaven friends. You have fixed their machine a few times, you know, Bert and Charlie… They should be here any moment."
"Y…Yes…" I stuttered as a thousand distressing memories flooded into my panicking brain. "I have met them. I think they have a J…J…Jones machine."

We walked into the *pit of doom*, along the narrow corridor that opened into the main sitting room or in this case, boudoir, now the sign on the bungalow made sense. It was dimly lit with several garish lamps dotted around the room, almost the exact copy of their Peacehaven friends. The lavish curtains were more like ball gowns draping over the windows and ominously closed. Sitting, no, half lying on a chaise-longue was another man-woman-thing, in a stunning full-length frock that must have been stolen from Barbara Cartland, complete with a crimson feather boa.

"Oh darling! You have arrived at last. We have been so looking forward to meeting you. Now come and sit down beside me and we can discuss our little problem."

"You know I only fix sewing machines, don't you?" I said in dread.
"Silly boy, why else would you be here? Now come and sit down. Queenie! Get the kettle on, let's all have a brew. Now, dear. Do you mind me calling you dear? Oh, of course you don't! We have a problem with our machine. It's over in the corner there, see it?"

I looked into the gloom of the corner and sitting there was an old Singer 29k boot patching machine.

"What on earth would you want with a boot patching machine?" I said sliding to the furthest corner of the chaise-longue, which seemed to be getting smaller by the second as Betty slid closer to me, flashing overworked eyelashes.
"Well now, that is for me to know and you to find out isn't it?" Betty sniggered.
"Whatever is that smell?" Queenie asked sniffing the air with a disgusted look on his face.
"Oh, I am afraid that is me, I have been fixing a machine at Hastings fish market this morning and the smell has clung to me."
"Clung, is an under-statement dear boy! You smell like an Egyptian brothel! And I should know." Replied Queenie, opening a window. I tried to ignore his remarks and examined the machine.
"I will need to know what sort of material you are sewing to set up the machine."
"Oh, in that case you had better see what we have been sewing." Betty rose from the chaise-longue like an ageing movie star, flicked her long gown behind her legs and sauntered off towards another room.

I took the time to weigh up the situation. Do I bolt or face the music?

They seemed harmless, just a bit colourful. I had to admit they did bare a striking resemblance to their Peacehaven friends Bert and Charlie and, although those two made my heart miss beats, they never got out of hand, so to speak. I seemed to remember one awkward moment with one of their hands clasped around my backside but, besides that, I escaped in one piece.

Yes, I thought, I would stay and sort out their machine. Well, they are paying me and that's what I do!

Queenie came into the room with a tray of tea and cakes and broke my thoughts. Things were looking up. He put the tray down on the table in front of me and started to pour out the tea from a beautiful lavish gold teapot. "One lump or two dear?" Queenie smiled holding a sugar cube over my teacup with a pair of silver sugar tongs.

"Just the one please."

"Bert speaks very highly of you, he should be here any moment, we are all going out for lunch at the Pavilion Tea Rooms. Have you been there?"

"Yes, it's a lovely place for a bite to eat," I replied, relaxing slightly at Queenie's easy manner.

"Now what colour takes your fancy?" said Queenie waving a hand over the tray of fondant fancies. "My favourites are the pink ones?" he added.

"I'll have a yellow one, I think."

"Good choice dear, my second favourite."

I settled down to my tea and fondant fancy and found myself relaxing as Queenie told me how they had met at the camp pantomime while doing National Service back in the 1960s. I could not imagine a stranger place for men of different persuasions to meet than in a gruelling National Service camp. Visions of the two of them putting on the pantomime ran through my mind. Men prancing about in female costumes! Taking more than a liking to their dresses. What a sight!

I had a mouthful of cake when Betty returned holding the item they wanted to sew on the Singer boot-patcher. Half of my fondant fancy sprayed across the room and I choked on the rest as I realised it was a **leather thong**.

"Silly boy! Now look what you have done." Said Betty stepping over the mess. "Queenie, grab the tea before he spills that too." I was still choking and spluttering when Queenie prised the teacup and saucer from my shaking hands. I proceeded to cough up crumbs as he whacked me on the back.

"I don't know," said Betty laughing, "Some people just can't handle their food."

"Don't expect me to clean this up," spouted Betty. "I am not getting on my knees in this frock.

 184

"I am so sorry I'll do it." I spluttered, trying to get up.

"Silly boy, leave it to me," said Queenie, going off into the kitchen to get a cloth, "I have cleaned up a lot of worse things than cake crumbs in my time."

"I feel such an idiot, I am afraid you just took me by surprise with that thong!"

"They are not for us, we are much too old for those uncomfortable things. But we have a market for them, we have sold over 50 this year alone, in all sorts of colours. Red is the most popular. We were going great guns until the needle broke last week and the machine has not sewn a stitch since. We have orders piling up so we asked around and that is when Bert and Charlie told us about you. How do you feel now? Cleared your lungs out a bit?"

"I'm feeling much better now." I said wiping away a tear. Betty handed me the leather thong. He could not help notice the look on my face as I examined it.

"Come on now, Alex. We all have to make a living…. Well a bit of money on the side anyway. Now you go and work your magic on the machine before those other devils turn up because when they arrive *all hell is going to break loose!* They do like to play those two"

I made it my mission to get the machine fixed and get out of the place before the *Peacehaven pair* arrived. But as I was just putting the last screw back in the machine, the doorbell rang. A cold shudder ran through me as the thought of Bert and Charlie and all their pranks ran through my mind. There was a commotion at the door as the four of the *femmes fatales* hovered around each other in excited greetings.

I heard Queenie say, "Come in, come in you two! We have someone here that you know and he has just finished a wonderful job on our machine."

In floated Bert and Charlie, not quite as dressed up as they were at home but still in make-up and heels. They must have been in their subtle going-out make-up.

"Oh My feet are killing me Queenie," said Bert. " These new shoes are a death to wear. Worse than glass slippers. But they look so elegant. They suit my narrow ankles don't you think? I don't suppose I could use your foot spa for a few moments to ease the swelling?"

"As long as it is only your feet that are swelling!" They all roared with laughter at Queenie's dirty joke and rolled into the lounge where I was trapped.

"Oh my! What has died in here?" I heard Bert ask as they walked along the corridor.

"That's Alex! He has been doing something fishy this morning," laughed Betty.

Like a rabbit that has had the ferrets set on him and there was no way out, I tried to play it cool and smiled as Bert saw me. "Oh Alex, you've lost weight, can't call you *chunky* anymore can we! It suits you, shame about your cheap aftershave though! You should try some of mine – *Pour Femme* by Hugo."

"Let me see!" Shouted Charlie, pushing into the room, which was shrinking fast. "Oh yes! Definitely a few pounds missing off you dear." He said examining me like a side of bacon at a butcher's shop and waving his hand in front of his nose at the same time. "You haven't caught anything nasty have you?"

Once again all four of them reeled with laughter. I laughed as well I couldn't help it. It was easy to see why the two couples got on so well with each other, they were like four sisters rather than four cross-dressing, overweight, bar-room bouncers.

"No, no, its just the fish, I have been on a diet for months now. It has been hell!"

"We know he has been on a diet," said Betty. "He spat out half of my fondant fancy all over the carpet earlier. Never swallowed a bite. Now that is what I call discipline! Mind you, it was only after I showed Alex the leather thongs that he had his coughing fit. Before that he was eating the cake like it was his last meal. Now, who is for tea? Queenie – you be mother and put the kettle on sweetie."

"Alex," Betty started. "We need your advice. We have been thinking of starting a singing group, the four of us. A bit like a *barbershop quartet* and we were going to change our stage names to suit. Charlie is going to become Daisy, Bert was thinking of Iris, I was going to be Bella, after Belladonna. You know? *Deadly nightshade* because I am *deadly on the dance floor*. And Queenie was going to be Petunia. Then we could call our group the *Flower Fairies*. Clever eh? I have seen some lovely organza fabric that would match a clutch bag I bought last month. Ooh! I can't wait to start making the costumes."

Flower Fairies! What a thought! I did think of offering the name *Ladybugs* as that was a more suitable description of them. It would be hard to imagine a more scary sight dancing around the bottom of your garden, than this quartet of overweight drag queens in skimpy, fairy costumes.

"Well, you will all have to dress the part as well. To match each other," I said, "you know, it could go with the act, all dressed as flowers." I secretly thought that one of them should obviously be called Pansy but said nothing.

"Yes! What a good idea," said Betty. "We could certainly add that as some continuity to our act. I must tell Queenie."

As Betty left the room Charlie said, in hushed tones, "We all agree except Betty who does not want to change his name. You know why they call him Betty don't you. He loves a little flutter on the G-G's, can't help himself. When he comes back, ask him who is favourite for the 2.30 at Goodwood today. He knows all the form. Mind you never wins a penny!"

"I heard that Charlie!" Betty shouted coming out of the kitchen with a foot massaging machine filled with water. "I won a tenner last month on *Bold and Beautiful* when it came in third at Chepstow."

"Well, besides that, you have not won a thing for months. Have you dear?"

"It's not the winning, it's the taking part!"

"You have got that *all arse about face* you twit, it's not the Olympics, it's a seedy bookmaker's down the High Street. I think you only go there because of that lovely young man behind the counter. And that's a peroxide rinse on him, if ever I saw one."

"Oh you are just jealous because he talks to me!" Betty spat back at Charlie with a sharp sideways stare. "One more word out of you dear and I won't let Bert soak his great lumps of meat in our spa!"

"Calm down girls," I said. "You're all getting in a 'tizz-was'."

I was worried that they might all explode into a catfight. "I think the name for the group is great and you only have to use the names for your act, not at home."

"Yes, of course!" Betty chirped up, "What a clever boy you are! We should have thought of that. Now where is my tea? I'm parched?"

Bert's feet slid into the spa and his face, that had looked like he had trodden in something nasty, changed to one of indulgent bliss. "Ah that feels so good." Bert said with pure pleasure resounding in his voice. "Just in time too as my bum's gone to sleep all down the left cheek." he added, leaning over to one side and massaging his left buttock.

Queenie came out of the kitchen with more tea and Betty sorted out my money.

"Would you like one of these to take with you dear?" Betty said holding up a bright, red thong with a depraved smile that could only come from a lifetime of teasing people. "No, no thanks, honestly, I don't think it will suit me!"
"Don't knock it until you try it dear." Betty retorted.

As I moved towards the door, with my tools, the four of them started to get excited. Bert lifted his feet out of the spa dripping water onto the carpet in his rush. Queenie almost dropped the tea tray in a rush to put it on the table. Charlie was already prepared, lingering by the hallway trying to whistle. And Betty was about to pounce.

There was a moment's silence, like the second before the starter's gun goes off for a race. I needed a diversion to get up the hallway to the front door. I remembered, only too clearly, the last two occasions that I had met Bert and Charlie and getting out of their house was traumatic to say the least. Getting your bum pinched by a 17-stone lorry-driver come flower-fairy was enough to put the willies up anyone!

"What a beautiful lamp." I said nodding in the direction of the light in the corner of the room while clutching my toolbox with a grip of iron. "Is that silk?"

The split second that they all turned towards the lamp was enough for me to get in front of Charlie. I was off at a fast pace, down the hall to the front door with a herd of wildebeest stampeding behind me. As I got to the door the group were hot on my heels, urged on by an enthusiastic momentum that could not be halted. I looked round as four huge shapes bore down on me in a panting rush. At the last second they tried to slow down but to no avail. Although they had managed to stop, the hallway carpet they were all on, had not. It was coming my way and carrying the four ugly sisters, all with looks of horror plastered on their faces. What a sight! I closed my eyes, braced myself and held my breath as they tumbled onto me in a mass of hairy arms, legs and wigs. I felt the rough bristles of one of them rub against my cheek as I struggled hopelessly beneath the pile.

"Oh, poor boy! Give him room to breathe," Charlie said as he tried to help me up. Bert was howling as someone had trodden on his toes in the mayhem. I looked up to see Queenie leering at me with a look that could sink a thousand ships and Betty, stuck behind the pack, was desperately trying to see what was going on.

"I'm OK. I must have tripped on the carpet." I lied, getting to my feet and clutching the handle of the front door with a grip so tight it would have throttled a goat. I wiggled around the bodies, arms and legs and squeezed through the smallest gap in the door that would, in normal circumstances, be impossible to get through. I had often heard how foxes, with a pack of hounds on their tails, escaped through tiny holes. Now I knew how they did it. I dragged my toolbox though the gap and was out of the house. The door flung open and four panting faces peered out at me. It was too late, I was up the path and away.
"Come back soon.... but have a shower first." Shouted Queenie, straightening his wig.
"Don't forget to tell all your friends where to buy lovely soft thongs from!" shouted Betty
"We will do a special price for you." Charlie was blowing a kiss in my direction and Bert was still howling in pain, clutching his big toe in one hand and leaning against the door for support.

If only I had a camera, I thought. The picture was priceless.

I was in a state of elation at managing to escape from the bungalow amazingly unscathed. Not even so much as a groped bum. Their disappointment at not grabbing my backside was hidden in a barrage of one-liners thrown to me. I smiled from the gate and waved farewell to the *Flower Fairies*.

I was riding on the crest of a wave. They had been the last call of the morning so now I could go home and clean up. Once again I had escaped.

I might smell of fish and be covered in make-up but, in the spirit of the true self-employed, I had a pocketful of money and was still alive.

I walked briskly along the row of bungalows whistling as I went. My toolbox, once again, brushing the side of my trouser leg as it swung. I was overjoyed. If I can handle four *flower fairies*, whose combined weight must have been around a thousand pounds, then I could handle just about anything life could throw at me. Now all I had to do was get home and have a shower and make sure I got rid of the make-up clinging to my face.

Part of the Hastings fishing fleet, that still earn their living from the sea.

EDIE'S STORY

The heat was unbearable, like wearing an electric blanket on a hot day it encased and smothered you. It was 2 am and I was leaning out of the window watching the night pass. There was no wind, just the stifling night imported from an old film like *Mogambo* or *Key Largo*. I can never sleep on hot summer nights. I toss and turn in restless slumber. But tonight something was going to happen, there was electricity in the air.

Nothing moved, no branch or leaf. The wind had disappeared into the blackness. All the noises of the day that blend and mingle to become a loud hum had disappeared and each noise of the night had become distinct. A car driving somewhere, the engine note rising and falling as the gears changed and it slowly faded into the distance. The bark of a dog from the estate below. The sharp cry of a fox looking for his mate. No stars, just black above and rows of yellow streetlights below, picking out the houses that lived under their nightly glare.

Something was going to happen. You could just feel it. There was energy in the air. I watched and waited, my face glistening from the unaccustomed tropical heat. Then it came. At first I thought I had imagined the leaves rustle because they started and stopped so quickly. I leaned further out and strained my ears. Then it came again.

A breath of wind ran through the garden. Like Odin's handmaidens, the Valkyrie, searching for those to be slain in some mystical battle. First one gust, then another. They slipped through the blackness gaining in strength and temper. The trees shook, the leaves rustled, and the wind washed over my hot face in a torrent of darkness before disappearing into the night. Then, once again, all was silent.

A street-light along the road started to flicker, throwing a pale yellow light along the pavement. Somewhere in the distance an owl made an uneasy screech. Once more the sticky night fell into a deathly hush. A hush so quiet you could hear the beat of your own heart.

I waited, staring into the sultry night. Suddenly a bolt of lightning burst from the heavens, lighting up the town in brilliant blue, followed by a clap of thunder as Thor's mighty hammer, Mjolnir, pounded the dry earth and shook the sleeping world below.

The thunder died away, rumbling off to find some other battlefield where the old gods still play. Then the rain started. Heavy drops, growing in strength. Splashing on the dusty leaves and bouncing off the ground. All around the air was filled with the noise of raindrops on roof tiles, on trees, on pavements, on patios and pathways. Gutters sprang to life, gushing forth water like forgotten springs.

The noise of the rain lifted the silence of the night like a thousand typists in a typing pool, tapping away on their keyboards in the darkness. For the first time in days a wash of cool air came my way. I smiled, lay back down on the bed and let the welcome rain lead me into sleep.

The next day the air was clean and sweet and summer had changed with the first cool morning of early autumn, leaving trails of mist over the warm sea. By the early afternoon I was flagging from the long, restless night. I weakened at the sight of the apple and blackberry pie that Edie put in front of me. I soon found myself sitting, eating and chatting to Edie about her early life in the sewing industry and her story was a cracker.

Edie – short for Edith – had left school at 14 and had gone to work in a Singer shop. Her father got her the job because he was a Singer man himself. Her first job was to sit in the front window of the shop and demonstrate the different attachments for the sewing machines. On Mondays the shop would stay open until 9 pm and Edie would demonstrate each attachment to a willing customer. Quite often with a small group of onlookers gathered outside.

If you came back and learned how to use all six attachments you would be awarded a certificate and a discount on your new Singer sewing machine.

By the time Edie was 16 she was working in a big London Singer store and she was already the proud owner of a 1951 Centenary Singer 201K awarded to her for her outstanding sales. It was this machine that I had come to service. She had the knack of putting customers at ease but she also had another asset, she was very pretty. A definite bonus if a couple came into the shop, the husbands were only too happy to listen to her sales patter. The Singer store was not only full of sewing machines but also the complete sewing package. From *haute couture* dresses to fabrics and every *Butterick* sewing pattern under the sun.

As times changed so did the selling. When Singer started promoting their zigzag machines, Edie would sit in the window doing appliqué stitch and create various patterns. Singer would send down blouses that had already been half appliquéd and Edie would copy the design onto the other half. When finished, the blouse would be sold in the shop and she would get an extra shilling for each one sold.

Having a pretty girl sewing in the window was great for business and as a bonus Edie got to choose which young man she would go out with. There were usually a few waiting for her on a Friday night after work.

By the time Edie was 18 she was working in a top Singer store. As the premier sales-girl out of a 20-strong team, she was picked to go to the *World Trade Fair* in Belgium.

Edie was amazed at the fair. It was held at a huge ultra-modern building that was like a starfish with restaurants in the arms and big show-floors full of every new product that the world had to offer. The product that stood out the most, in Edie's mind, was the amazing *Kenwood Chef* that looked like it was from outer space.

Singer had their very own special promotion as well. They had produced a machine that half a century later would still be declared as one of the finest Singers ever made, the **Singer 222k Featherweight**. They were taking the opportunity at the *World Trade Fair* to push the sales of this little beauty.

In Belgium, Edie was trained in the manner of basic French lessons. *"Good morning, would you like us to send you a new catalogue?"* was the extent of her lessons! If the customer showed an interest Edie would then take them to one of the many other showgirls on her stand who could speak their language. Singer had the top sales girls from every European store on their stand to promote their machines. All the girls were dressed in a Singer blouse, with the *Singer* monogram across the pocket, and identical skirts.

The back wall of the stand was made up entirely of Singer 222k's. What a sight that must have been!

Imagine Edie, a young woman never having been abroad before coming from an austere 1950s England that was still recovering from rationing, being carted off to a country she knew nothing about. To the very latest up-to-date, ultra modern *World Trade Fair*. Her homesickness was overtaken by her amazement at the new world she had entered.

People came from all over the world to marvel at the latest inventions on display. Edie was allowed one phone call from her hotel every week and she would eagerly wait her turn to phone her mum and tell her all the exciting things that had happened during the past seven days. The most exciting moment of the show was when Queen Juliana came to the stand and spoke to her about the pretty little black sewing machine that was later to capture so many hearts.

One other incident happened which I have heard of before. She was demonstrating the new Singer zigzag machine when her hand slipped and the needle came crunching down on her finger. The needle broke in her finger and she had to go and get it bandaged up. Almost a year later she kept scratching a little lump that had appeared on her big toe. One day the lump broke open, and to her utter astonishment, the tip of the needle came out of it! The needle fragment had spent a year travelling painlessly around her body before coming to the surface at her toe.

Edie spent six months at the fair promoting the *machines of the future*. While there were many new machines on display, none came close to the perfection and lightness of the Featherweight. It took the show by storm and beat all the competition, with their heavy cumbersome machines. Although Edie adored the 222k and demonstrated it to many customers, she could never afford one herself for it was far more money than she could pay on her salary. The machine would have cost her 12 weeks' wages in the 1950's.

Many times she saw a 222k leaving with a new owner and felt a pang of envy.

At the end of six months it was time for Edie to go home. She was given a delicate silver bracelet with a pretty little Singer engraved on it with her name.

When Edie arrived back at the London store, her father had prepared a surprise presentation. On a Saturday afternoon, after the store had closed, all the staff gathered around. Her father, who worked at another London store, came in with a large box. He made a speech in front of everyone saying how proud he was of her and how she had been the top sales-girl at the world show. He then handed her the box.

She opened it and inside was a brand new, perfect Singer 222k Featherweight, courtesy of Singer and her father. Edie burst into tears as everyone cheered and applauded. Her father hugged her and whispered in her ear, "You deserve it my girl! I am so proud of you."

It was the best Saturday of her life. Even today she remembers her father's face swollen with pride as she wept tears of joy after opening her gift.

"What a great story Edie!" I said, "and the pie was scrumptious."
"Would you like to see my special baby Alex?"
"What, the 222k? You still have it?"
"Oh yes, that machine will never leave my side! I am taking it to the grave with me. Wait here a moment, I shall fetch it!" Edie almost skipped out of the room and returned several moments later with an old box and a big smile.
"My God! That is the original packaging the machine came in. Isn't it?"
"Yes, I have saved everything." Edie said removing the black box from its carton. She opened the lid and pulled the 222k out tenderly as if it were the *Crown Jewels*.
"Wow! That is the best Featherweight I have ever seen, have you ever used it?"
"Oh yes, once a month I take it out and wipe it over then run a piece of material through it. Just to keep it running. And a drop of oil now and again if it sounds off. My mum tells me when it needs oiling, she has an ear for it."
"How old is your mum Edie?" I asked, working out with a little mental arithmetic that Edie must be in her sixties.
"She is coming up 97 this month. The rest of the family call her the *coffin dodger*. We have decided that she will never die because death will never find her. She is hardly at home two days in a row. She tells us all that a good tipple of brandy before bedtime keeps the doctor away. But we suspect it may be before lunchtime and dinner time as well! Still, she thrives on it!

So who are we to judge?"

I helped Edie put her precious machine back in its box like a baby in a crib. The machine that held a thousand memories of her younger years was slipping back into its pampered resting place. I hoped God would not mind allowing Edie to bring her machine with her when she made her final journey. You could just imagine her walking along the *Pearly Way*, with her black box, towards St Peter at the gates of Heaven.

Well, they may allow hand luggage – you never know!

"Edie," I said "It has been a privilege to hear your story, to eat your wonderful pie and to see the most perfect Featherweight in Sussex. Oh! By the way Edie, if my wife phones and asks if you fed me, please just deny everything. She has got me on the diet from hell. Last night she even cut an apple into long chunks to look like French fries, just to make me feel better. But I can tell you, steamed fish and apple fries just ain't the same as good old *battered cod and chips*. Another thing I have learnt is that it does not matter how you prepare fruit and vegetables, there is still nothing like a good steak! I think that you can boil, fry, mash, bake or nuke – celery and guess what, it still tastes the same.

"Alex," Edie smiled back, "If your wife phones I will forget everything. It is one of the advantages of age."

One of my typical calls to a horse rug machine near Ashburnham.
I often work on farms around my area.

AUTUMN

Oh autumn in England is such a time,
She shows all her glory looking so fine,
The smell of the harvest, the breeze from the sea,
Oh England at autumn is the only place to be.

The swallows rise high on thermals that flow,
Corn fields sway in a countryside aglow,
Colours of the forests dance all around,
Mother nature's beauty, a paradise found.

Cotton wool clouds play up on high,
The animals busy storing winter supply,
Chestnuts ripen and the mushrooms arrive
The starlings gather, the woods are alive.

Soon will come winter and dark gloomy nights,
When we shut our eyes to relive these sights,
Oh autumn in England is such a time,
She shows all her glory looking so fine.

A. I. A.

AUTUMN APPROACHES

"You won't tear Lizzy away from the garden fence now. She has lost her tongue chatting to our neighbour. She will be half-an-hour, if a minute!"
"No problem Ned. I can get on with the machine while she is chin-wagging. Is it still in the spare bedroom?"
"Sure is me lad."
"Well I'll get started."
"Good lad. I'll swing the kettle over the fire for a brew."

I was at a small cottage, on the back road to Robertsbridge, called the Old Coach House. It was probably the original coach house that served the large inn on the main A21, London road. For many centuries, travellers from the ports of Rye and Winchelsea and the landing points off the Hastings beaches would have taken this route to our great city. Many properties I visit have these sweet, rather quaint names. *The Old Toll House, the Old Forge, the Old Priory, the Old Police House.* I've never found one, yet called the *Old Brothel.* Maybe they are all still in business!

Lizzy's machine had had a rather a nasty shock the week before my visit. Just after dawn, Ned had walked across the bedroom to open the curtains. He tripped over the power lead to the sewing machine and sent the Necchi flying off the table.

After careful examination and a detailed discussion with Ned, over a cup of tea, we decided that the only thing that would bring the machine back to life was a force in the opposite direction to the one that damaged it.

Ned and I went around to the back garden and, while Ned held the machine on its end, I used his large club hammer to move the top shaft back into position. One perfectly placed wallop was all the machine required to free it up.

As the thud of the hammer rang around the garden it broke the noisy chattering coming from Lizzy. Lizzy and her neighbour threw horrified looks our way. Ned assured me that the silence was just a temporary loss of sound and dialogue would resume shortly.

Ned whispered to me, "She is like an old newspaper hack, never lets the facts get in the way of a good story. Mind you Alex, we must keep her happy, if mother's happy, then everyone's happy."

"What on earth are you doing Alex!" Exclaimed Lizzy as she hoisted her apron up over her waist and moved towards me like a large battleship about to engage the enemy. "Don't worry I have done this a thousand times before. It is the only way we are going to get your machine working again. You will just have to trust me!"

"You men are all the same! Fix anything with a hammer." She said sliding up to us and berthing her wide frame next to me. "Alex, if you do a good job I have just baked a wonderful gooseberry pie and I will give you a slice. It is still warm. Ned picked the gooseberries this morning."

"You're on! Get the pie ready. I will have this machine sounding so sweet you will enrol it in the church choir."

"Lizzy makes the best pies in the district." Ned butted in proudly. "I have not been able to do up my waistcoat for 20 years because of them."

Thoughts of hot gooseberry pie encouraged me to get the Necchi running as if it was its first day out of the factory. By 9.30 am all four of us – her neighbour was not going to miss out – were sitting in the garden tucking into slabs of moist, warm pie topped with cream.

By 10 am I was back on the road, heading towards Robertsbridge Community College to service a dozen machines. The early autumn day was lost in mist, the beautiful High Weald countryside was hidden behind a soft haze that had just started to burn off. It would be gone by lunchtime and the heat of a late summer afternoon would blaze over the ripe crop fields.

The vineyards and hop fields, that I knew so well were nowhere to be seen. I had witnessed the mist come off the Downs the night before. It had stayed on the high ground like an encamped, invading army. So thick that you could not see twenty paces in front of you. As the day cooled into evening the mist moved downwards, silently rolling over the countryside as if it had been given its marching orders for the invasion of Sussex by night. It flowed from the Downs like dry-ice off a stage, I had been out cycling and had seen it coming. A thick cool wall of silence enveloped the road as it flowed over me on its secret mission to steal Sussex away in the twilight hours.

Along the roadside verges little signs were stuck on wooden poles, *Game and Country Fayre* at Michelham Priory, *Music Spectacular* at Battle Abbey, *Festival of Transport* at Hellingly, *Horam Flower Show*, the *Laughton Country Fayre*, the *Medieval Festival* at Herstmonceux Castle and the *Firle Place Horse & Country Show*. Harvest fayres and flower shows abound in autumn. The August Bank Holiday is probably the busiest holiday of the year for country events.

There would be a thousand dedicated vegetable and flower specialists all referring to their *Royal Horticultural* handbook for rules and regulations. I knew old Vic would have been tying little pebbles to his giant runner beans to get them to grow that little bit longer.

A prize at the local flower show gave you respect and envy for a whole year, something well worth the effort. At the Rushlake Green summer show a few weeks ago, I picked up a wonderful toy *Grain* sewing machine from the *bric-a-brac* stalls, ate a slab of homemade cake, had a throw on the coconut stall and listened to the band play on the sunny afternoon, while watching and applauding the kids races. I even peeked inside the flower and fruit tent when all were forbidden during the judging and generally enjoyed myself. A village show is one of the great rural pleasures that England still boasts.

I parked and walked through the damp, high grass to the prefab building at the back of the college. Dozens of little seeds stuck to my wet, leather shoes in the hope of reaching fresh soil. A thousand little cobwebs, all perfectly formed, lay on the grass like pale handkerchiefs dropped from childrens' sleeves and my footsteps left a wriggly trail in the dewy grass.

Yes, I thought, autumn was on its way – and the countryside knew it.

By late morning I was on the road again. My next call was in Friston, back down near the coast. It was an easy drive along the twisty lanes of East Sussex. I lazily meandered along with the radio playing jazz tunes. They were having a Glenn Miller *big-band revival* that was a dream to listen to.

My mind was wandering as I drove, catching odd sights and images thinking about them for a while until another scene caught my attention. I was annoyed that a Bristol bank had pulled the rug out from under a loan on the *Trug Shop* in Herstmonceux. The shop that made trugs since 1830 and was the oldest business in the village. I am sure they had supplied Queen Victoria and her children with the special little garden baskets which would soon be gone. A developer would step in and grab the shop in the high street. I wondered what Reg, the old trug maker, would do instead of sitting outside the shop working the wood in his special way. The way he would stoke the chestnut planks and feel the grain before deciding which piece would fit the basket best. He would sit outside the shop working his trugs always stripped to the waist. His cheerful wave, leather bronzed skin and eagle eye may soon be a thing of the past.

To commiserate with Reg, I stopped and bought a punnet of *Kent cherries* that were being sold on the roadside along with plums, greengages and strawberries. Kent cherries are the best cherries you will ever taste! Each one explodes with sweetness and flavour as you eat them. I sat and devoured my cherry lunch by the Jack Cade memorial near Heathfield. It is the place where, legend has it, he was captured.

The whole area around Cade Street is ripe with history and, although Cade Street actually existed before Jack Cade came into this world, there is no doubt that it is because of him that it will be remembered. Many areas were named after the families that lived in them, so it is more than probable that Cade, being a family name, could have been used for generations before the most famous of all the Cades left his footprint on history.

****

Jack Cade was a man of some importance in East Sussex. There had been unrest in the country for some time and temperatures were running high. In 1450, less than 20 years after Joan of Arc was burnt at the stake in France, Henry VI was up to his old tricks raising taxes once again. It was the final straw. Cade and the countryside exploded with fury.

Henry had apparently surrounded himself with *sycophants* and *yes-men*, he handed out land and favours to the select few. He knew little of what was happening to his subjects, and cared even less. Jack Cade and a few other ringleaders stirred up a huge rebellion of some 30000 working men and marched on London. Henry sent his troops out to meet the uprising. They clashed at Sevenoaks, so named for the seven oaks that grew on the common. Henry's troops were defeated with pitchforks and scythes. Then the rabble of Sussex and Kentish yeomen marched on to the capital.

When they arrived, although their blood was up, the horde had lost sight of their objectives. They did not receive the welcome from Londoners that they had expected. The Londoners were not happy to see them at all. What was happening in the countryside was of little concern to Londoners as long as their food and goods arrived.

After a few minor skirmishes in the capital, mainly around Blackheath, Henry met with the ringleaders and promised them whatever they wanted. Jack Cade was sceptical because he knew the King was on the verge of madness. He wanted to continue his quest for fairer taxes but his colleagues thought it better to grab what they could and leave. The rabble floundered, dispersed and drifted back to their smallholdings and farms.

Henry seized his chance and put a huge bounty on Cade's head. Jack Cade changed his name and fled, but it was only a matter of time before he was caught. While making for the coast with the sheriff of Kent hard on his heels, he was cornered in a garden near Heathfield. Legend tells that he died from his wounds before he could be put to death in London. A ceremonial beheading on his corpse still took place at Newgate, his head preserved and placed on a spike on London Bridge. His body quartered, wrapped in oil and tar cloths to stop it from rotting too quickly, then the parts taken to each of the centres of unrest around the country and displayed as a warning to others.

A monument stands today, near Heathfield at the spot where he first fell all those centuries ago. A hero of the people, who met a gruesome death for his beliefs. He was a man out of his time, centuries before the first unions. People say that Shakespeare later wrote of Cade and his earlier counterpart, Watt Tyler, in his plays. Cade was a believer in a state that no king could ever imagine, one that put the people first. It took another 500 years for his dream to be realised.

****

By early afternoon the sun was blazing down and I was at my next customer in Friston, along a dirt track that leads to one of the most wonderful viewpoints in our area. The track by Friston Church leads to Crowlink, a small hamlet of houses that nestle in the side of the downland, a mile from the main road. Once past the hamlet it is a short walk to the cliffs.

At the cliffs you see one of the most wonderful sights that any eye could behold. Sweeping views of open rolling downland, cliffs and sea. In the distance lies the Cuckmere river estuary where many a smuggler came to shore before they built the Coastguards' Cottages there.

It was around this spot on the Downs, in December 1944, that the last known sighting of the worlds most famous bandleader, Glenn Miller, was made. His plane was heading into the mist out over the English Channel towards France. Glenn had left for Paris on a small Norseman Plane, a light plane made of linen and wood. He had waited for days at Twin Wood Farm Air Base for the thick fog to clear so that he could get to Paris to entertain the troops. In the end he grabbed a lift on the small plane that was taking an officer to Paris. It was to be his last flight.

No one yet, knows the exact spot where the plane went down, but there is evidence to suggest that he may have accidentally been hit by allied bombers that were jettisoning their bombs over the Channel after an aborted mission. The big-band leader, whose songs crackled over the airwaves as couples danced around the floor, disappeared into history and left us a priceless legacy of *Pennsylvania 6-5000*, *Chattanooga Choo Choo* and many other wonderful tunes.

The day had gone well, the machines had all been successfully repaired and I had no hitches. The sun was shining, birds were singing and all was well with my little corner of the planet. My Kent cherry lunch had been the perfect way to balance the gooseberry pie I had scoffed earlier. Tomorrow was the dreaded weigh-in again. Yana would be ceremonially jotting down my weight on the note pad once more, like she had done every week, religiously, since the diet started. Many months had passed since my first shock on the scales. The weight that had secretly crept onto my hips had reluctantly packed up and left. I still had a long way to go but at least I was heading in the right direction.

On leaving my customer I stopped to pull out into the main traffic heading to Eastbourne. At Friston there is a small pond right opposite the early-

Saxon flint church of St. Mary the Virgin. The church has a unique *Tapsell Gate*, that is hinged in the middle. It makes a splendid entrance to the church and frames the graveyard beautifully. There are several similar gates at churches in our area, like Jevington, but none exactly like the Friston one. There was a lonely grave there when I was a kid marked simply *washed ashore.*

The churchyards around this area hold sailors that have come to grief on the treacherous rocks off Beachy Head, once called *The Devil's Cape* by fearful seamen. One of the old vicars, the Reverend Jonathan Darby Esq, became so incensed by the needless loss of life around the rocks at Beachy Head that, empowered with God's strength, he dug steps through hundreds of feet of chalk, down to the beach and enlarged a cave there to shelter sailors. One night he saved the entire crew of a sinking ship. It was the Church's responsibility to find and bury the drowned sailors. Many a priest would beachcomb, looking for the bodies. A piece of a body was called a *Gobbit* and still needed a Christian burial.

In olden days, when an extension was built onto an old flint church, it would stand out a mile. To disguise the new parts the builders would make up a weak mix of diluted animal manure and spread it all over the new work. Within a few months it was almost impossible to tell where the new work had been. Harry Cherry used this very same technique on the East Dean church extension. It worked like a charm.

Back to my story. As I was pulling into the traffic I looked across to Friston Pond and suddenly remembered a funny incident that happened there. One summer long, long, ago when I was still a young and willing worker ready to earn some extra cash, an old friend hired me to clear the weed from Friston Pond. It is a yearly job to keep ponds clean and free from unwanted weed.

I was busily working away at the backbreaking job of heaving out great lumps of weed when my workmate, Ray Attfield, suggested that we take a rest and have a pint of beer down at the Tiger Inn in East Dean. The idea, on a hot afternoon was well received. Before long we were sitting on *the green* outside the Tiger, *wetting our whistles* with a welcome cold brew. We had a couple of pints each and walked the long, hard climb back up to the pond.

Within an hour or so all I wanted to do was fall asleep. From that day on I have never drunk during a working day. Ray and I were *half-cut*, dragging the weed out so slowly that the stuff almost died of old age rather than our efforts. While I was weeding, I heard someone calling to us and looked up to see two old dears standing by the edge of the pond. They had come up to ask us what we are doing. Always one for a laugh, Ray told them that we were clearing the pond to make way for a concrete *roller-skate* rink. They were very popular back in the '70s.

As the two bemused ladies wandered off we both had a laugh and carried on. We thought nothing more of it. As I was clearing the pond, I bumped into several bags down by my feet. As they were not weeds and I was drunk and half-asleep, I left them in the pond. My excuse being we were told to clear out the weed, not sunken rubbish. Later Ken Warner, who had hired us for the job, pulled out the bags, only to find that they were stuffed full of stolen silver from a robbery along Friston Ridge!

Our two old ladies, unbeknownst to us, had gone off and caused pandemonium. They had phoned just about every person they knew in the village to find out about the skating rink. The rumour spread like a prairie fire. It was out of control. By the end of the day, an emergency parish meeting was called and everyone had gathered to find out what the hell was going on. About 11 pm I was woken by a call from a furious Ken saying he had just spent an hour on the phone to Commander Blah-Blah Fortescue the third of the Fourth Bengal Tigers, retired. Well, something like that. Ken had to assure the commander that it was all a little joke by the two young lads he had employed. He had promised that he would take them to task over it.

I listened to Ken as he gave me an ear-bashing and I apologised for our drunken slip of the tongue. I hung up the phone and laughed until I cried.

Needless to say the pond is still there but we do not get asked to clear it out anymore!

The beautiful Friston church of St. Mary the Virgin. This gate is a unique Sussex portal, a Tapsell gate. This church is right opposite Friston pond and the path to Crowlink.

Brown Bread Pony Sanctuary. What a wonderful place to spend your days. Just along the road from the sanctuary in Brown Bread Street is the fabulous Ash Tree Inn. No finer food is served in East Sussex.

*An old cannon in my prawning grounds off Beachy Head.
Was it lost during the Battle of Beachy Head in 1690?*

*One of the last surviving beach huts that once dominated Eastbourne's beaches. Many were turned
over, filled with pebbles and laced with barbed wire to hinder any invasion during WWII.*

Top of Lewes High Street. Note the house next to the Brewer's Arms, it is the house that the revolutionary Thomas Paine once lived in. He penned part of the American Declaration of Independence. Thomas Edison called him 'The Real Founder of the American Republic.' "The Harder the conflict, the more glorious the triumph." – Thomas Paine.

The Horse & Groom in Polegate High Street.
If you ever want a good bit of pub grub, you will find few prettier places to eat. Just to the right of the road sign is the horse drinking trough, now full of flowers

LAST CALL

It had been a long day but a short year. The weeks had turned into months and time had once again stolen the year away from my grasp. The golden colours of late summer would soon blend with the turning leaves and the countryside would once more glow in her glorious shades of autumn.

The day's work had gone smoothly and I had one last stop at East Dean to fix John's fish-net making machine. In my mind I thought that I would get the machine sorted and to take a break up at Beachy Head, on the point of the downland, just to soak up the wonderful sunshine for a few minutes before returning home. You seldom see any signs at Beachy Head, for they are all pinched by visitors. They should sell reproduction ones at the gift shop.

It is only the English that call some of the highest points in our land *Downs*. In reality the word Downs comes from an early Anglo-Saxon word *dune*, meaning hill.

It did not take long to fix John's machine. As I made my farewells I knew I would be back before the end of the year. The strain of sewing lead line to rope would wear the best of machines. It does not take many months before his heavy industrial gives up thumping through the lead rope and grinds to a halt.

With all my calls finished for another day I headed past Birling Manor to Birling Gap where you can find the only steps down to the beach between Seaford and Eastbourne. You walk down the steps and are transported to a natural landscape as wild, dramatic and beautiful as any place on earth. It is unique, and a great spot for prawning. It is also home of many a shipwreck, at low tide you can still see the remains of the *Oosla* and the *Thomas Gilby* ship that made its way safetly from Australia in 1876, before coming to grief on Flagstaff Point. There is even the remains of a WWI German submarine. Haven Brow – one of the places near Birling Gap – has a name so deceptive to the dangers that strong tides and rocks pose.

I made my way up over the glorious downland towards Belle Tout, past the notorious suicide spot where many a life has ended tragically. The Belle Tout lighthouse (French for *beautiful outlook*) was made from Scottish granite around 1828 a few years before young princess Victoria ascended to the throne. The granite was hauled all the way from Aberdeen then loaded onto ox-carts and heaved across the Downs to a spot around 90 feet from the cliff edge. Today, because of erosion, Belle Tout sits near the cliff edge like a cherry on a half-cut Belgium bun.

However, things are not as precarious as they first seem, Belle Tout is now on rails and can be slipped away from the cliffs as further erosion takes place. One of our local councillors raised the money to have the work carried out and was promptly accused of some sort of scam. If it were not for his vision and determination, Belle Tout would have fallen into the sea. Rather than criticism he deserved a pat on the back. Belle Tout was replaced with the lighthouse at the foot of Beachy Head that stands some 144 feet high and is painted red and white, in St. George's colours. The Beachy Head lighthouse was built from Cornish granite in 1902. In fact, this year it celebrates is centenary.

Combine harvesters were being followed through the fields of corn by tractors pulling carts for the grain. The harvesters were pouring wheat from their long giraffe-like necks and dropping bales of straw behind as they lumbered through the fields in clouds of dust. Not long ago 30 men would be hard at work doing what one machine does today. Gypsies, travellers, farm hands, neighbours and casual labourers would all come together for the harvest to work the land in its most plentiful time.

I parked in one of the many car parks at Beachy Head and sat for a while overlooking my superb hometown of Eastbourne. A herd of cattle were moving slowly across the open green pasture in a timeless scene, the young following close behind the mothers in case they stopped and so could feed. A peregrine falcon swooped passed me, low to the ground with strong wing beats, heading for the corner of the harvested field. It must have spotted a field mouse or some other creature that had been disturbed by the farmers.

It is little wonder Norman invaders long ago called this place Beachy Head, well originally they called it *Beau Chef* or *Beautiful Headland*. There are few places that I have ever visited that could hold this title with such pride. It is one of those places that you just want to touch with your hands. To get out of the car and drop to your knees, to feel the downland turf and drink in the heady aroma of the wild flowers, that mix with the sea breezes in a heavenly cocktail. Legend tells us that William, Duke of Normandy used the high, white cliff faces to chart his course towards our shore when he had decided to come and claim his inheritance and teach us table manners.

****

Eastbourne snuggles at the foot of the South Downs at the edge of a huge sweeping bay that ends at Hastings some 15 miles away, as the crow flies. At one time, the bay was far larger and the water extended miles inland. When the Romans landed, they built *Pevensey Castle* on the seashore. Now its walls, where once the tide lapped each day, lay several miles inland. The castle, besides a few ghosts, still boasts the finest Roman castle entrance, or gate, in Britain.

In 1690 there was a great naval battle here, *the Battle of Beachy Head*. The French were once again after British soil and along with a landing of troops in Ireland, Louis XIV's admiral was attacking the English fleet off Beachy Head. Over 8000 cannon roared in anger off the coast as two of the mightiest sea powers at the time, waged war. It is difficult to imagine on such a serene and peaceful day that the waters of this headland would have boiled with falling grape shot, and the air would be full of the stench of gunpowder and burning sails, as men screamed and battle raged. Louis lost the battle of the *Boyne* in Ireland to William who, just two years into his reign as king of England then secured his protestant rule over the country. However, although the French lost at *Boyne* they were winning the battle of Beachy Head but fate played a strange hand in the battle. When the destruction of the British fleet looked probable, the French admiral suddenly called off the attack and headed home, something that no one could understand or explain. When he arrived back in France, the French admiral was dismissed in disgrace. And the British fleet! Well, they survived to fight another day.

From Beachy Head it is easy to see why Eastbourne has been popular with so many visitors. The view evokes an image of old England. Grand houses and church spires rise above the town skyline that ends so perfectly with the interruption of the sea and a line of large hotels along the seafront.

Eastbourne still paints a picture of strolls along the promenade and meals at fine restaurants. Quaint, civilised, elegant, an image of yesteryear that can cope with the modern world in which we live.

The Germans did their utmost to remove Eastbourne from the map. Bombing her relentlessly on their trips to and from London. Eastbourne was the first town to be bombed on the mainland in the war and at least 11,000 houses were damaged or destroyed. Although Eastbourne lost some irreplaceable Victorian architecture, her soul survived. I remember the last bombed church, in Cavendish Place being demolished. It had been left for decades untouched, a reminder of troubled times. Along the Downs there are still arrow-straight lines of bomb craters that can be clearly seen in the grazed fields. In the marshes and wetlands, in corners of fields and in woodlands hide forgotten *Pill Boxes* – small concrete and brick buildings with enough room for a few determined soldiers to hide and fight. They were the last line of resistance to an invading force. In truth they would have been of little use against the might of an invading German army and their *Blitzkrieg*.

It was just off Beachy Head in March 1940 that *SS Barnhill* was bombed. I seem to remember from Yana's grandparents, that it was being towed to a harbour when it broke in two and sank, just beyond Langney Point. The boat was so close that it could be reached at low tide. This provided a bonanza for some of the more daring locals, including Yana's grandmother, Iris, who stocked up with the tins of food that floated out of the broken hull. Iris told me one of the other goods it was carrying was typewriters, which once the salt water had got to them became useless. Each night at suppertime, she would sit down with her family and have *tin surprise*. The reason it was a surprise was that the sea had washed off the labels so Iris never knew if she was having tinned peaches or stewing steak until the can was opened. The broken remains of the *SS Barnhill* are still visible at low tide. It was one of my favourite fishing spots as a child.

The list of celebrities that have visited and stayed in Eastbourne is as long as your arm. Beside all the dukes and duchesses, actors and tennis stars we have had many Royals. Our present Queen, the Queen Mum, both Edward VII and Edward VIII, George VI and a list of princes and princesses over the years. There have been a handful of other notable visitors. Lewis Carroll (of

Alice in Wonderland fame), Beatrix Potter, T. E. Lawrence the one and only Lawrence of Arabia, Alfred Lord Tennyson, Anna Pavlova the gifted Russian ballerina, Nelly Melba, and Sir Thomas Beecham. George Orwell (Eric Blair) went to school in Eastbourne and many say his masterpiece 'Animal Farm' was based around Chalk Farm at the end of my road in Willingdon.

Debussy penned *La Mere* while staying at the Grand Hotel. Sir Arthur Conan Doyle visited – the man who brought the first forensic detective – Sherlock Holmes, to life. Rudyard Kipling came. He was the first writer to receive the Nobel Prize and who loved the Sussex Shires with all his heart. Then there was the misunderstood, brilliant author and feminist, Virginia Woolf. Hillaire Belloc with his breathtaking descriptions of the Downs and beligerant attitude, would hurtle down the Sussex lanes on his Penny Farthing bicycle. A. A. Milne, who brought so much pleasure to millions of children with *Winnie the Pooh*. Sir Edward Elgar who penned the inspirational *Land of Hope and Glory*. The dramatic and beautiful photographer, Lee Miller. The composer of *The Planets*, Gustav Holst and the Swedish nightingale, Jenny Lind who stole Isaac Singer's heart with her beautiful voice and seductive smile.

Ernest Shackleton lived in Eastbourne for many years and brought his ships '*Quest*', '*Endurance*' and '*Nimrod*' to the town. It was Shackleton that made one of the greatest sea journeys in history, when he took his men on an epic 800 mile rescue trip to South Georgia from Elephant Island, when his ship, '*Endurance*' became lodged in the ice.

Charles Darwin stayed here, pondered and wrote some of his earth-shattering book *On the Origin of Species by Means of Natural Selection*. My mother nearly bought the manor house that the artist Mabel Lucie Attwell lived in. Mumsie was outbid at auction and missed the chance to own a piece of early Eastbourne history. Ocklynge Manor is reputed to have once been owned by the Knights Templar.

Eastbourne, with her ancient roots and modern facilities, breeds enthusiasm and success. The superb Eastbourne College taught men like Frederick Soddy, Nobel Laureate in chemistry, and adventurers and pioneers like Fredrick Minchin who, in 1927, set out to cross the Atlantic in the aircraft *St Raphael* and vanished into history.

The list is endless. They came to our pretty town, some just to visit the theatres or tennis tournaments, some to watch cricket at the Saffrons or just to soak up the sea breezes and refresh their souls. Some to walk the prom and see the famous Carpet Gardens and the pier and to listen to the band play at the Bandstand. The beautiful Carpet Gardens are laid over the remains of an old Roman palace and some mosaics still remain hidden beneath the flowerbeds.

Yana's grandfather, who was responsible for growing the plants that would be displayed in the gardens, once told me that they used to lay the flower beds out in a typical Roman pattern to mimic the mosaics below. During the war, while he was busy in the Far East, his beloved beds were turned over to the growing of vegetables for the war effort. And huge *Bofors* anti-aircraft guns lined the promenade. Once back, he soon had the flower seedlings grown so that the gardens could be replanted in all their glory.

The war changed Eastbourne forever. For example, just one beach hut survives from the hundreds that once littered the beaches. The bathing huts that were part of *old Eastbourne*, would be lowered into the sea by horse and the person inside would then step out for a swim. The horse then pulled the hut back again after their refreshing dip in the revitalising waters. During the war, the huts were tipped onto their sides and filled with sand, then rolls of barbed wired spread out in between them to hinder any invading troops.

How things have changed! Today we greet our neighbours across the water and join with them in a common market, working together for a better Europe.

Eastbourne still has something special. She is a big town that retains all the heart and charm of a small seaside resort. A town whose street names still tell of the people that built her and lived here. The top hat'n'tails and evening gowns may be a thing of the past but Eastbourne, the quintessential Victorian town, my hometown, the town I love – still lives up to her title as the *Empress of Watering Places*.

House martins were passing low over the downland in their hundreds, darting, twisting, creating a short, sharp, noise like a tiny firework erupting as they shot past. They were feeding on the wing, occasionally calling to their young that were playing with their new acquaintances. The smallest of the swallow family were making their way along the coast towards Dover for a short crossing to the continent to winter in warmer North African climes. They travelled in a never-ending string of birds along the old migrating paths, little changed since the dawn of time.

Skylarks were gathering in flocks, some of a hundred or more, rising and falling like waves into the grasses. They had finished their eternal summer songs for another year. Now only calling in short sharp bursts. It would be many months before their energetic songs once more filled the South Downs with vitality and enthusiasm. A farmer was following his two border collies as they rounded up sheep that grazed on the rich downland grasses. They would be off to the markets of Sussex. Their short but contented lives nearly over.

In olden days, once the last bale of straw was stacked and the grain safely stored in the granaries, all the farm hands came together for a celebration, a *harvest festival*. Bread made from the first grain would be baked and all the people that had helped in the hard work of harvesting would celebrate the bountiful year. Wholesome loaves would be broken open and jugs of ale and wine filled. A riotous party would go on late into the night with singing and dancing.

Around 1840 a West Country vicar with a small parish, I think his name could have been Hawker, wrote to his parishioners asking if they would like to celebrate their festival in his church. Hawker was a visionary, a poet, an opium smoker and all round controversial figure. I seem to recall that he was even married to a woman some 40 years his junior. He managed to gather his Cornish flock to his church at Morganstone. His parishioners brought what they could spare for the needy of the area and celebrated under God's roof, probably with a bit less alcohol. So started the religious service of *harvest festival* that continues to this day.

Hawker waited until he was on his deathbed before converting to the Roman Catholic faith, something he could not have done until his dying day for he was a happily married man. Had he done so, earlier in life, he would have had to part with his dearly beloved. But as he was dying he could no longer stay with his wife anyway hence joining the Catholic faith was no hardship for either of them. Now that is what you call timing!

****

I soaked in the view that I had seen a thousand times and never tired of. I knew it would not be long before the full harvest moon would be chasing silent shadows over Sweet Brow and the soft autumn dew would raise the tasty, plump, white-capped field mushrooms that I adore. I drew a deep breath, as if to capture the moment one more time, started up my faithful Land Rover and pointed her towards home.

The car had travelled the roads so often she seemed to drive herself down the steep, twisting, drive that drops through the heavy woodland on the side of the downs and comes out at the top of the promenade at my old school of St Bedes.

St Bedes, the school where yet another slightly eccentric English teacher taught his class that there were really only three dates in English history worth remembering, 1066 William's landing at Pevensey, 1666 the great fire of London and 1966 when England beat Germany at football – to win the World Cup!

The End

Kent cherries, simply the finest cherries in the world, and sold along the roadside when in season.

People often hear me talk of an English Cream Tea and wonder what all the fuss is about. Well this is a jam scone filled with whipped sweet cream and strawberry jam. There is no more pleasant way to spend an afternoon than sipping tea and scoffing scones.

GLOSSARY

240 volts [AC]	The standard distribution voltage of electricity supplied in much of the world. Unlike with 110VAC a good jolt can kill earthed humans
A27	One of the many numbered roadways in UK prefixed A for arterial and M for motorway (restricted access)
Ack-Ack guns	Anti-aircraft guns, from First World War army slang
Aerial	Antenna
Aga	A type of large cooking stove, from *Svenska Aktienbolaget Gasackumulator* the original manufacturer
Anderson shelter	Simple half-buried backyard bomb shelter. Roof made from curved corrugated sheet metal with lots of soil, from the hole beneath, covering it. Useful protection from blast and shrapnel
ANZAC	Australia and New Zealand Army Corps, from the abbreviation stencilled on stores in the 1914-1918 war
Biddy	An old woman
Bickies	Biscuits, a cookie
Bill Sykes	A character in Oliver Twist, a story by Charles (John Huffam) Dickens, 1812-1870
Bishop Barnaby	Sussex slang for a Ladybird
Bishops Finger	Great Ale, enough said
Bisto	A brand of powdered gravy thickener and flavour
Blackberries	Known as brambles in US
Blitzkrieg	A *Lightening War* or ferocious military assault to bring about a swift victory.
Brits	Originally a short form of *Britons*, the inhabitants of southern England, now any person from the United Kingdom
Buckingham Palace	One of the monarch's residences, this being in London
Bungalow	A one-storey house

Chamberlain	(Arthur) Neville Chamberlain, ineffective conservative, pacifist, prime minister of Great Britain 1937-1940.
Channel	The English Channel separates the UK from Europe
Chelsea Pensioners	The popular name for the In-Pensioners of the Royal Hospital, Chelsea, founded by Charles II. It is maintained for selected veterans of the regular army, since 1692. The men appear at functions in red and black 17th century army dress uniform
Coffin Dodger	A very old person
Conker	A horse chestnut swung in a children's game to break that of another contestant
Corn	Any edible grain, but especially wheat, in England. Not maize
Cuppa	A *cup of tea*
Daddy Longlegs	A small web-spinning, family *Pholcidae* with long thin legs. Also *daddy-long-legs*
Daniel Defoe	Author of *Robinson Crusoe* and others, 1661-1731
Demobbed	Demobilised, or discharged from the military at the end of hostilities
Desert Rat	*Desert Rats* are, strictly, British 8th Army and Commonwealth soldiers who defended Tripoli for a period in WWII. They were under the command of Montgomery and their emblem was a desert rat.
Doodlebugs	German pilotless, V1, flying bombs, from the warbling sound made by the ramjet engine. When the fuel was exhausted the craft lost flying speed and stalled into the ground
Druid	One of an order of priests in Celtic tradition
East Sussex	A county of the United Kingdom, previously the eastern part of Sussex County
Edwardian (period)	During the reign of Edward VII, 1901-1910, characterised as opulent or ornate. Now regarded as leisurely and self-satisfied
Fayre	Quaint English for *fair*, an open-air sale and entertainment area. Also for *fare*, food

Fete	An outdoor function, usually, to raise money for charity, church or school, combining the activities of a bazaar and fair
Foot and mouth disease	A contagious virus affecting cloven hoofed animals characterised by vesicular eruptions about the hoofs and mouth. A recent outbreak in UK is said to have cost US $10 billion
Flicks	Cinema
Football	In UK soccer. Not any other game, of football, that are all given their official names
GCSE	General certificate of secondary education, a year-11 attainment
Great Britain	England, Scotland and Wales together with Northern Ireland
Green	Village grassy area
Guildhall	In London the hall of the corporation of London used for ceremonial occasions, a trades or city hall
Hawthorn	Small tree of genus *Crataegus* cultivated as a hedge and for the brightly coloured blossom and red fruits
Homer Simpson	Cartoon character on television
Horse Guards	Since 1969, The Blues and Royals (Royal Horse Guards and 1st Dragoons), a unit of the British Army given today, largely, to ceremonial
Indian Pale Ale	A beer, brewed by top-fermentation. Ale was any hop-free beer *Archaic*
Jim-jams	Pyjamas
Kip	Sleep, originally military slang
Knapped	Broken up into small pieces with hard blows, chipped
Knocked for six	An old cricket term when the ball was whacked so hard, it left the playing field.
Lance Corporal	First, non-commissioned, rank above Private in British army
Land girls	A group of conscripted young women, in World War II, whose job it was to work the fields in place of the men
Land Rover	A popular utility vehicle or 4x4 in UK.

Lay-by	A rest area at the side of a road, usually without anything other than parking space
Lbs	Abbreviation for pounds, the weight measure, *qv*
Mad dogs and Englishmen [go out in the midday sun]	Song by Noel Coward, *1899-1973*, that relates how English people are wont to do silly things in the tropics.
Mall, The Mall	A broad thoroughfare alongside St James Park, London, leading to Buckingham Palace from Charing Cross
Marks and Spencers	Own brand clothing and food retailer chainstore
Mobile phone	Cellphone
Minor 1000	Small, 1 litre car made by Morris Motors Limited. Forerunner to Morris or Austin Mini. www.geocities.com/MotorCity/Track/2508/bmc2.html
Monte Carlo	Mediterranean principality with a casino that has attracted the aristocratic or nouveau riche English to gambling for many years
Mum's the word	A World War II exhortation to keep one's mouth shut, now part of the vernacular
Nags Head	A notional pub
National Trust	An organization for maintaining and preserving historic buildings and such ephemera. *The National Trust, 36 Queen Annes Gate, London SW1H 9AS*
National Service	Compulsory military service for young men, conscription, the Draft, and the term for its organisation
Parcel Force	Delivery division of what was called *Royal Mail* postal service
Persia	Iran
Plague	An epidemic disease of high mortality. Known as *The Black Death* in the 14th century, *The Great Plague of London* in 1664-1645
Pound	A monetary unit in UK, depending on exchange rates about US$1.50. Also a weight measure in Imperial system, about 454 grams
Pub	Abbreviation for a *Public House*
Pye-Core	Wry name for corps in British Army, also Pie Corps

Queen Mum	Elizabeth Bowes-Lyons, wife of George VI and mother of Elizabeth II, a queen dowager
Rat and Parrot	A notional pub
Rolly	Alex's dog, a Patterdale terrier
Rommel	Erwin Rommel, 1891-1944, German field marshal and commander of forces in North Africa in World War II, *The Desert Fox.*
SAS commando	Special Air Service, an Army special force unit
Scone	A baking powder biscuit
Shilling	A small coin in English coinage before decimalisation, 7 cents
Sloe berry	Fruit of *Prunus spinosa*
Smidgen	A very small amount
South Downs	A range of low hills in southern England stretching from Dorset to Sussex. Also, *Southdown*, a breed of sheep known for their strong short wool and particularly for their lamb meat
Speckled Hen	A beer
Stone	A measure for a person's weight, 14 pounds, about 6 kg
Sussex	Originally a Saxon division of England, literally South Saxon land, previously a county of South Eastern England
The Strand	A London thoroughfare, from Charing Cross to Fleet Street
The Red Arrows	An aerobatic team from the Royal Air Force, flies Hawk aircraft
Twitten	A narrow alley, *Sussex dialect*
Vaseline	A brand of petroleum jelly, a light refined petroleum wax suitable for human-skin application
Wattle and daub	Rods and twigs woven together and plastered with mud and manure to create a wall
Weald	Archaic term for open or wooded country. *The Weald* formed a wooded district of what are now counties of Kent, East and West Sussex, and Surrey that is now a grassland agricultural region

Wellie-tossing	A sport where waterproof (gum)boots are thrown for distance. From *Wellington's* a knee-boot popularised by Arthur Wellesley, 1st Duke of Wellington 1769 – 1852
Wetting your whistle	An old term for having a drink.
Whirling dervishes	A Dervish is a member of any of a number of Muslim asthetic orders, some of which carry on ecstatic observances such as violent dances and pirouetting, thus a *whirling dervish*
Winnie the Pooh	Title of a children's book by AA Milne *1882-1956*
Winston Churchill	Sir Winston Leonard Spencer Churchill, British politician and writer, prime minister 1940-1945, 1951-1955. Noted for leadership in World War Two.
Women's Institute	An institution for country women to gather socially to do charitable works and for self-improvement
World War II	War between Allied powers and German axis (mainly Germany, Italy and Japan), from September 1939 until August 1945 according to those in the United Kingdom. Also WWII

Well that's it folks the third in the Random Threads trilogy all done and dusted, now where do we go from here?

For information on how to order a copy of this book go to:
http://www.sussexsewingmachines.com
htttp://www.crowsnestpublications.com

 223

DO NOT GRIEVE

When my time has come, there is no need to wonder where I'll be,
No hushed chimes of Westminster will be calling out for me,
But the downland turf is where my spirit shall run free.
The soft green hills of Sussex will hold my heart for all eternity.

I'll be with the Seven Sisters as the first rays of sun spill over the sea.
With the mists that hide the tempest's roar off Devil's Chimney,
High above Holywell I'll follow the warm thermals that gulls soar upon,
And the blast of east wind that howls over Frost Hill with its icy song.

I'll be with the spring flowers that carpet the slopes at Michel Dean,
With the mermaids purses on Falling Sands where wildness rules supreme.
No, do not stop to grieve for me, never doubt where my heart will be,
For I am here with the wind, the sun, the sand and the sea.

I'll be with the summer rain that gently falls on Whitbread Hollow,
With the running tide that the seaweed at Cow Gap tries to follow.

****

And when you stand at the towering cliffs that rise to Beachy Head from the sea,
Gaze across this timeless landscape and know my heart is here my soul is free.

ALEXANDER I. ASKAROFF